T0193760

STRATEGIC APPROACHES
FOR TURNING MALAWI
FROM POVERTY TO A WEALTHY NATION

Learn the Turnaround Strategies for
Transforming Malawi Economy

Kingstone Ngwira

authorHOUSE®

AuthorHouse™
1663 Liberty Drive
Bloomington, IN 47403
www.authorhouse.com
Phone: 1 (800) 839-8640

Published by AuthorHouse 02/23/2018

ISBN: 978-1-5462-3003-8 (sc)
ISBN: 978-1-5462-3004-5 (hc)
ISBN: 978-1-5462-3005-2 (e)

Library of Congress Control Number: 2018902198

Print information available on the last page.

Contents

Dedication

To the Almighty God, the source of all true visions and sustainer of all dreams.

Acknowledgements

Let me start by saying that, this book is a culmination of my research work from various studies that have been conducted many years ago. My research is a function of the experts of numerous people who helped to organize and contribute towards the aforementioned components in various areas. I heartily congratulate them for their efforts.

First I would like to thank the Almighty God, the source of all true visions and sustainer of all dreams who has marvelously helped me to move from one level to where I am today and I wish to thank Him for current successes as well as those that are to come in my future glorious years.

My particular thanks go to my lovely wife Pastor Shannira, my children: Pastor Prince and Gift, my relatives and my friends who have fully supported me in all my undertakings throughout my studies and research projects. I am grateful to my spiritual father in the Lord Apostle Dr. Madalitso Mbewe for his continued encouragement, spiritual and moral support as well as for his guidance.

It is practically impossible to acknowledge the help and guidance of everyone who assisted in my research work components but mention must be made to distinguished academicians such as Vice Chancellor of Lilongwe University of Agriculture and Natural Resources {LUANAR}, Prof. George Kanyama Phiri, Prof. Yohanne Nyasulu, Prof. Jan Botha, Chairman of Council for Mzuzu University {MZUNI}, Prof. Brown Chimphamba, Prof. Kuthemba Mwale, Dr. Sam Safuli and at Pentecostal Life University {PLU}: Prof. David Kamchacha the Vice Chancellor for Pentecostal Life University (PLU) who have worked tirelessly to have this book a success. God will reward their efforts for their professional guidance and encouragement and support in many fronts.

And last, but not least, I would like to thank the Board of Trustees of Pentecostal Life Church International {PLCI|}, Corporate Printing and Packaging Limited {CPPL}, Exploits University, Pentecostal Life FM and TV for their untiring efforts. The support to make this project a success is acknowledged with gratitude.

Preface

This book is a must read book for everyone that would want to see Malawi transformed from poverty to a wealthy nation. The discussion in this book falls into the study of public sector management and economics full stop, Specifically it aims at providing strategic approaches and turn around strategies for Malawi to move from poverty to become a wealthy nation. Malawi needs a vibrant economic system that would create its own wealth from all subsectors. When the principles and concepts of strategic management presented in this book are deliberately followed, it is envisaged that the economy can start creating wealth. Many economists say that economy is composed of individuals {Households}, firms and the state. This means that the individuals and the firms form micro-economics and the private sector while the state forms the macroeconomics and the public sector.

The Public Sector Management (PSM) is about managing public services. On one hand PSM is concerned with those services which are mainly or completely funded by taxation and which are not sold to customers at a price which produces profits. There is also no competition in enticing customers away from their competitors {Duren 2010). Because these basic features of a market such as competition and the market structures are absent and many principles of management which apply in the private sector are absent.

Other principles such as equitable treatment and allocation of resources according to needs are also absent in market processes of decision-making and management. On the other hand the private sector is perceived to be an engine of the economic growth in terms of its contribution to the labour market, procurement of raw materials, production of goods and services that are consumed by the community and the payment of taxes to Government department such as Malawi Revenue Authority {MRA}.

In the past two decades, Malawi has witnessed slow down of business transactions to the extent that some companies have been closed. Additionally, there has also been retrenchment of people at all levels, lower buying power due to continued depreciation of Malawi Kwacha, low tax collections, higher levels of borrowing by Government both locally and internationally, high inflation and interest rates that have contributed to the down fall and closure of businesses especially in the small and medium enterprises {SMEs}.

The solution to these challenges rest for Malawi to seriously rethink of reviewing and implementing its long term development strategy backed up by well defined long term implementation goals that will see both private and public sector being adaptive, revolutionized, reconstructed, created and recreated in some instances and not forgetting the stakeholder management approach. To achieve this goal comes the three players {individuals [Households], firms and the state} that form the economy to participate in running the economy. This is a call for new vibrant public and private sector management and partners.

Kingstone P. Ngwira

Introduction

Geographically landlocked, Malawi is one of the least developed countries in the world. Malawi's economy relies mostly on grants from foreign donors. Agriculture is the most important sector of the economy and accounts for 80 percent of the labour force and 80 percent of exports. Serious deficiencies in the public sector, telecommunications and infrastructures are an obstacle to growth. According to Reserve Bank of Malawi report (2016) the Gross Domestic Product (GDP) in Malawi expanded 2.90 percent in 2015 from the previous year. GDP Annual Growth Rate in Malawi averaged 4.34 percent from 1994 until 2015, reaching an all time high of 16.70. This means that our GDP is not promising.

Malawi faces four key policy challenges. A study commissioned by the global oil firm Puma Energy exposes four key challenges that policy makers in Malawi should work on. The study dubbed "the changing face of Africa,' conducted by the London based independent economic consultants called Llewellyn Consulting, singles out the exchange rate, natural resource management, structural transformation and employment as four main policy challenges strangulating and dogging Malawi (Nation Online 2013). Malawi is still facing the four policy challenges till to date and this calls for search of strategic approaches and implementation strategies for wealth creation.

According to the study findings, Malawi faces a daunting task of ensuring a stable exchange rate, which is one of the most key determinants of the economic growth – as measured by the gross domestic product (GDP), among other fundamental economic variables. The report says as the economy enters lean season – when demand for foreign exchange is excessive on the few supply of dollars and other foreign currencies available on the market-both importers and exporters are keeping their fingers crossed to the movement and to the subsequent strength of the local currency. With this development policy makers such as central bank or Reserve Bank of Malawi (RBM), finds it tough to manage the few supply of foreign reserves and ensure smooth importation of key goods and services.

The report further John Llewellyn, one of the co-authors of the report points out that Malawi also faces the policy challenge of improving transparency in the way it is managing its natural resources which include the huge discovery of minerals in recent years.

On the employment the report findings explain that Malawi faces the challenge to reduce working poverty as well as youth unemployment which currently is wide bemoaned among most local economic commentators, recently being the Lilongwe - based Centre for Social Concern (CfSC).

The public sector is going through reforms in order to improve its performance in all sub sectors. In many respect the public service can be described as "non productive" and drain resources from the "wealth producing" sectors of the economy.

Malawi needs a vibrant economic system that would create its own wealth from all subsectors. It is envisaged that when the principles and concepts of strategic management in respect to strategic approaches as well as strategies for turning Malawi from Poverty to a Wealthy Nation being presented here, based on the research findings of my research are deliberately followed the economy will be vibrant and can start creating wealth. This is a call to move from free market economy to mixed economy.

The mixed economy is the type of economic system that allows all the three players that form the economy: individuals [Households], firms and the state to participate in the running of an economy. In the free market economy the individuals and the firms participate in the economy with little or without the state involvement or intervention.

Part 1
CREATION OR RECREATION?

CHAPTER 1

Wealth and Poverty

THE CONCEPT OF WEALTH IS CRITICAL and it is important that we think and talk about it because it provides a platform for all players in an economy to contribute towards making our country move from poverty to a nation that is wealth. In an environment characterized by political instability, growing globalization, escalating competition and rapid social and technological change matters about how our country can become wealthy would be increasingly vital to success.

From Poverty to a Wealthy Nation

States that wish to generate and improve wealth in an economy should develop deliberate policies that should facilitate wealth distribution at individual, business or firm and state levels. Therefore it goes without saying that state policies that affect a vibrant economic system in an economy should often be scattered throughout state government and do not fall completely within the purview of economic development. Malawi policy makers should ask these questions as they consider policies to promote an economic system that will promote wealth creation.

- What role can the public sector and private sector play in the state's current economy?
- What will the main players such as individuals, firms and the state need to be so that they are successful contributors to a health state economy?

In answering these two questions and in pursuit to wealth creation at individual, firm and state levels the state [public sector] as a key player should focus on these key policy areas:

- Tax Policy and Compliance
- Access to capital and financing mechanism
- Strong Fiscal Policy
- Promotion of State Programmes to the Malawi Society
- Building Regulatory Infrastructure
- Business Registration and Licensing
- Entrepreneurial Education
- Recognition of Private Sector as an engine of the national economy in terms of its contributions towards the provision of employment, procurement of raw materials and other inputs, operations and production of goods and services that are consumed by the communities
- Security Regulations and
- Promotion of specific programmes or policies that would address such needs

The road from poverty to a wealthy nation is the bedrock of wealth creation at the aforementioned three levels of an economy. This means that the responsibility of creating a new Malawi is for everyone. Additionally, according to Khomba [2002] the negative factors that would hold our country from enjoying include: the poor strategic planning processes; lack of vision amongst managers and leaders; poor work ethics; poor fiscal policies; poor business infrastructure; massive fraud and corruption; heavy taxation; general macro-economic instability; lack of management and leadership skills; lack of technical skills and innovations; use of inapproriate technology in our business processes; inadequate middle-level managers and lack of entrepreneurial spirit. By facilitating this dynamic and complex environment, the state can position itself to be attractive, competitive and resourceful public sector player in the economy.

Malawi has one of the best vision and mission statement in the vision 2020 document and most countries have indeed come and copied and contexualize in their countries. This document has so many policies. Our problem in Malawi is implementation. To this end more discussion has been more on issues of implementation of the policies and strategies with performance feedback. Therefore the implementation of short, medium to long term planning is very critical if Malawi is to realize the desired vision.

This is a call to change. It is this change that will see our country increase productivity, efficiency and effectiveness, solve emerging problems, deal with crisis, revolve, respond to changing technological demands and be competitive.

Many business commentators say that value creation perspective recognizes critical elements towards the creation of value for an organization. It is the aim of every company to engage itself in operations that add value to products and services for ultimate corporate sustainability. The value creation perspective is responsible for the transformation of inputs from different stakeholders into valuable products and services for final consumption.

Another important factor under the value creation is the intellectual capital. Thus the intellectual capital contributes directly towards organization value creation.

This takes us to the adding value processes and practices that include the deployment of new techniques such as the total quality management systems such as just-in-time systems and electronic commerce. According to Laudon and Laudon {2012} computerized systems such as automated database and filling systems and transmission systems have been proved to be of value adding towards increased efficiencies and effectiveness as well as reduction of costs.

Now the question is what does Malawi need? Creation or Recreation? Re-creation is Strategic change dictated by external events that usually threaten the existence of the organization and thus demand radical departure from the past. Change in leadership, values, culture for example takes place in this kind of change. Re-creation" on the other hand, is defined very differently. The other definition of re-creation that I came across consisted of three simple words—three simple words that speak volumes: "to create anew. To re-create means *to create anew.*

Malawi needs both creation and recreation. Creation in this case will help emerge new thinking and doing things more differently than before. The starting point could be to craft a clear strategic vision. The Bible is very clear on this" {Where there is no vision the people perish – Proverbs 29:18; KJV}. The vision that Malawi needs must be long term say 30 to 50 years. Research findings by Khomba (2016) have revealed that over the past two decades Malawi has been witnessing slow down of business transactions and closure of some of its very important companies. Khomba {2016} points out that this business contraction and massive closure of various companies has brought in so many socio-economic ills and evils among Malawians.

The general business contraction has culminated into massive layoffs of the working class people thereby generating low purchasing power, high interests and inflation rates, low tax collections, huge government borrowings, high rates of insecurity ending up with even more companies closing down. This experience has become a h disastrous consequences for the entire Malawi economy. The aforementioned ills that Malawi is facing require both creation in some areas and recreation in certain instances.

The Nature of Poverty

Poverty can mean different things depending on who is doing the defining. Poverty can mean shortage of money to buy the essentials that people or families need to support themselves. Defining poverty solely in terms of income or subsistence levels does not seem to capture the entire meaning of the concept. It is important to say that people with a culture of poverty produce very little wealth and receive very little in return. They have a low level of literacy and education and generally do not participate in the national welfare agencies. To this end poverty is not only an adaptation to a set of conditions but also tends to perpetuate itself from generation to generation.

Children born into the culture of poverty absorb the basic values and attitudes of this subculture and are not psychologically equipped even to take advantage of more favourable conditions or better opportunities that may occur in their lifetime. They tend to remain in the culture of poverty because it has become a way of life for them and not just a condition to be overcome. This concept has important implications for public policy measures designed to eliminate poverty.

The other way to look at poverty is a cycle, rather than in terms of a culture. The poor get sick more than other people, live in unhealthy conditions, have inadequate diets, cannot get descent medical care or a good education. Thus they cannot get and hold good-paying jobs to earn a decent income, which means they cannot afford good housing, medical ca re and a decent education. Poverty becomes a vicious cycle that tends to perpetuate itself, but the cycle can be broken into somewhere. If poor people could be given good jobs, for example, and receive the extra training and attention necessary to keep them, they might be able to climb out of poverty, breaking out of the cycle. This view of poverty has other implications.

The argument between those who think that poverty can best be eliminated by providing jobs and other resources and those who feel that cultural obstacles and psychological deficiencies must be overcome as well as ultimately an argument about social change, about the psychological readiness of people to respond to change, and about the role of culture in change. The advocates of resources are not concerned explicitly with culture, but they do make a cultural assumption: whatever the culture of the poor, it will not interfere in people's ability to take advantage of better opportunities for obtaining economic resources. They take a situational view of social change and personality: that people respond to the situations-and opportunities-available to them and change their behavior accordingly. Those who call attention to cultural obstacles, however, are taking a cultural view of social change, which suggests that people react to change in terms of prior values and behavior patterns and adopt only those changes that are congruent with their culture.

There are many factors related to poverty, including national, regional and personal factors. National factors include a downturn in the overall economy, which means that jobs, particularly unskilled jobs, are hard to find. Many people slip below the poverty line in periods of recession. A change in the nature of jobs available also relates to poverty, as unskilled jobs disappear with the advent of automation. Regional factors include slumps in a local economy that can be brought on when the major employer in the area fails to win a large government contract. Such contracts pump a great deal of money into a local or regional area. There may also a decline in the demand for locally produced goods and services. Regarding personal factors, there are five kinds of poverty properties that accrue to individuals: health; capability; motivation; personality and social economic status.

Handicaps, either physical or mental, make it difficult for a person to get a job, as does having a disease or an injury. Lack of a decent education or training is a factor in earning a decent income. People may also suffer a poverty of motivation because of blocked goals and frustration. They may not have been socialized into the basic value system of society and this may not share the same work habits as the dominant groups in society. Low social status relates to mobility, which tends to keep a person on the bottom of income scale.

The ability of a person to utilize or mobilize whatever personal resources he or she has available in an effective manner will help determine the nature and extent of relative poverty or prosperity. These personal factors are related, of course to national and regional factors as these latter factors provide an environment that is conducive or not conducive to the utilization of individual resources.

Because of poverty, some people are disadvantaged from the start of the race for the rewards society has to offer. They have at least one hand tied behind their back. They are never able to compete effectively and unless helped in some way simply fall further and further behind to constitute an underclass that is rooted in severe deprivation.

These people need some basic kind of help if they are ever to become productive human beings able to overcome the disadvantages of poverty. Only thus will equality of opportunity become a reality for them as well as for other, more fortunate, members of society.

The Nature of Wealth

From observation in some cases, the market system offers large rewards to winners of the competitive race, but it can also impose severe penalties on some of the losers. Those losers often fall so far behind that they end up in a seriously deprived condition. They have such small quantities of resources at their disposal that the market places a very slow value on what they do have to offer. The market system often promotes wide disparities in income and wealth, allowing the haves to mass increasing wealth and have-nots to fall further into relative poverty.

Often people end up in this condition through no fault of their own, since poverty is most likely a function of slack labour markets and general economic and social conditions. During the depression, for example, there are simply not enough jobs to go around, even for skilled workers who are willing and able to provide for themselves. Even in prosperous times there are sometimes not enough jobs for young people and others who have not had a chance to develop skills and ability they do have. And there are never enough good-paying jobs for people with severe physical and emotional handicaps who could still be productive to some degree. Finally, technological progress destroys the livelihood of many people almost overnight.

An unregulated market system can produce inhumane results, locking some people into a vicious cycle of poverty and preventing them from ever really entering into the race for the rewards society has to offer. Poverty can become a vicious cycle that is perpetuated from one generation to the next. Children grown into conditions of poverty have a high probability of remaining in poverty because of lack of good education, poor health, psychological depression, and more all of which places them at a severe disadvantage to people born into better conditions. Such disadvantaged people do not have much to offer employers and thus the market paces a low value on their services.

Poverty cannot be ignored by a society that proclaims democratic values, insisting upon the worth of all citizens and the equality of their political and social rights. Our commitment to freedom of speech, equality of suffrage and equality before the law rests on a broader commitment to human values that is violated by the persistence of economic misery in an affluent society. Almost all modern industrial societies have some kind of welfare system designed to altar unequal market outcomes through public policy measures. Such outcomes are unacceptable and are changed by a system of transfer payments that takes money from some groups in society through taxation and gives it to other groups in the form of benefits. Modern industrial societies also have programmes designed to help disadvantaged people gain education and training so they can have something valuable to offer employers or can start their own businesses to compete in the marketplace.

Workfare: Providing Economic Opportunities

One approach to the problem of poverty is to try and increase the range of economic opportunities available to poor people so they can help themselves out of poverty and work their way into the mainstream of society. Such programmes are based on the assumption that poverty is a condition to be overcome, not a cultural phenomenon and that poor people need assistance to break out of the cycle. This assistance can take the form of helping disadvantaged people become more employable in the marketplace, providing help for starting small businesses by providing economic opportunities particularly to minority entrepreneurs and building plants in disadvantaged areas to provide income and jobs for the community.

Disadvantaged people are shut out of many employment opportunities. Public policy measures aimed at eliminating discrimination in employment are not necessarily going to help them. What is needed to bring them into the marketplace is some effort to help them obtain the skills and experience necessary to get and hold employment. The emphasis of public policy must be placed on programmes to equip them with the skills, abilities and habits that are fundamentally necessary to compete for a job in the marketplace. There are both public and private sector programmes directed toward this purpose.

Minority Business Enterprises

Another approach to creating equality of economic opportunity is through the development of minority businesses. This approach involves giving minorities in this country special assistance in establishing businesses, forming capital, finding markets for their products and building managerial class. From this effort, the minority community should obtain a substantial measure of social and economic benefit.

8

The goal of this approach is not to eliminate discrimination from the employment opportunities in the institutions of society but to promote the development of more economic institutions owned and operated by minorities themselves.

CHAPTER 2

Wealth Creation Conceptual Frame Work

IT GOES WITHOUT SAYING THAT AS A NATION we all want to do better by staying wealthy, rich and abundant. And we are fascinated as well as envying those countries that are already there. The question is how did they do it? What magic did they use? How can we do it too? The simple truth is that wealthy countries tend to understand and do things the rest of us do not. This section codifies what those behaviours are so that we too can choose to be wealthier. The basis of the rules is that these are the things I have researched wealthy countries do. This means that if we do like them, we will become like them. This actually does work.

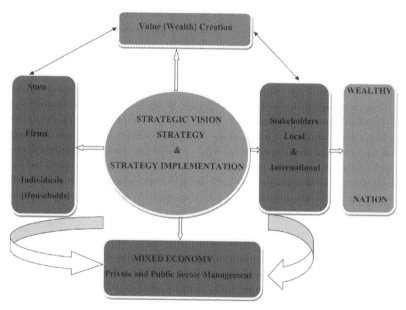

Figure 2:1 The Conceptual Framework of Wealth Creation

Source: Ngwira {2012}The conceptual frame work presents the circular flow that leads to a nation to become wealthy. Let us look at it in detail.

Entrepreneurs create products and services. They are usually the source of most new ideas in the economy. For example, Steve Jobs and partners created Apple computers n their garage and made computers a household item using technology that some big companies didn't see the value of. Entrepreneurial companies usually grow quickly and are responsible for much of the job creation in our economy. They take risks where big companies won't, and change where big companies won't.

'Profits' simply mean that the output of a business was more valuable than the input, which means that something of value to the economy has been created. There isn't much point in pursuing a business without profits (you would be no better off than when you started – or, if you have losses, even worse off). The profits are always either invested in new businesses or spent – and both of these activities help the economy.

Interest is the cost of borrowing money. If, for example, you want to start a limo company, and the interest rate is so high that the payments for your limo are so big that you can't possibly make a profit, then the limo business won't go ahead. If interest rates are high for the whole economy, lots of businesses won't make a profit and will start to shut down. Profits won't be made, and spending and in-vestment will decrease, which is not good for the economy. How much is too much? Really big profits mean that there is a lot of demand for that company's products. Others will want to get into the business and more companies will rush to fill the need. Competition will eventually force prices down. Take computers, for instance. The price was very high to start, but lots of companies started making them, and the price keeps falling. So, from an economic point of view, there is no such thing as "too much."

The Other Side of Entrepreneurs

Are there any drawbacks to cultivating entrepreneurs and entrepre neurship? Is there an —upper limit for the number of entrepreneurs a society can hold? Italy may provide an example of a place where high levels of self-employment have proved to be inefficient for economic development. Research reveals that Italy has in the past experienced large negative impacts on the growth of its economy because of self-employment. There may be truth in the old saying, "too many chefs and not enough cooks spoil the soup.

The right wing uses the —job creator argument to push the position that increasing taxes on the rich will burden job creators and deter from future job creation. The argument by Blodget and Hanauer opposes this position in an attempt to show that we should increase taxes on the rich and reduce taxes on the real job creators – the consumers. This is another common case of filtering economics through a political filter in order to validate a preconceived bias. Let's see if we can't filter our economics through an economics filter to arrive at a logical conclusion.

Although we did not realize it at the time, my wife and I found that the initial financing plan became a key component in building our personal net worth to a level where we are now able to create and endow a major medical research centre. The success of our first dream is making our second dream possible.

The person doing the work must have an incentive to do a good job and to be successful. If you are going into business, you must believe that you have the ability to make your dream happen. I sincerely believe I could accomplish the same thing today.

Investing in the Future Several investors, including doctors who were then retired or thinking of retirement, used a portion of their riches to endow chairs at the universities they had attended and to create foundations to make gifts to other worthy causes.

State Level

It is expected that entrepreneurs should contribute to growth and employment creation in advance, emerging and least developing economies alike. There are two major caveats however: First is that for entrepreneurs to play appropriate role, the role of the state remains important, if not more so than be-fore. Strong states as regulators and gatekeepers, play a particular vital role. In the absence or appropriate rules of the game entrepreneurship may result in undesirable social outcomes, including corruption, crime, speculation and financial crises and may worsen the vulnerabilities of people during natural disasters. The second is that while entrepreneurship may arise economic growth and material welfare, it may not always result in improvements in non-material welfare. Pro-motion of happiness is increasingly seen as an essential goal.

The question that comes to mind is why would an increase in entrepreneurship at first lead to an increase in national happiness? Entrepreneurs create jobs, and we know that un-employment is a major and significant cause of unhappiness. But we also know that entrepreneurs also associated with lower national happiness. This could be when most entrepreneurs are not so by choice but by necessity. Lastly, in every entrepreneurial society one may observe more and wealth ine-qualities and more variability in entrepreneurial performance. People in more unequal societies tend to report lower levels of happiness than others. Thus entrepreneurs may spur economic development if appropriately supported by the state. And entrepreneurs may also make nations happier – but only up to a point. As nations become happier their need for entrepreneurship seems to decline.

The Role of the Government in Entrepreneurship

An entrepreneur requires a continuous flow of funds not only for setting up of his/ her business, but also for successful operation as well as regular up gradation/ modernization of the industrial unit. To meet this requirement, the Government (both at the Central and State level) has been undertaking several steps like setting up of banks and financial institutions; formulating various policies and schemes, etc. All such measures are specifically focused towards the promotion and development of small and medium enterprises.

In many countries Governments set up institutions to support businesses with a view to promoting, aiding and fostering the growth of micro, small and medium enterprises in the country, with a focus on commercial aspect of their operations. It implements several schemes to help the MSMEs in the areas of raw material procurement, product marketing, credit rating, acquisition of technologies, adoption of improved management practices, etc. The other important policies for the sector relate to: excise duty; foreign direct investment approval and Labour laws.

What role should Government play in promoting Entrepreneurship?

Do you think government's direction should be around a) Access to Capital such as Grants, Loans for seed capital b) Simplification of their Policies and Proce-dures c) Public-Private Partnerships d) Create and manage competition by pro-moting a Public Sector Units e) Help with Diplomatic channels or something beyond?

Value Creation

The value creation recognizes critical elements towards the creation of value in an economy. The value creation is responsible for the transformation of inputs from different stakeholders into valuable products and services for final consumption {Khomba 2016}.

Mixed Economy

Mixed economy is the economy that allows all the three aforementioned key players to participate. The State represents the public sector while the firms and the individuals represent the private sector.

Local and International Stakeholders

Generally the local and international stakeholders focus on the recognition of the contributions of both public and private sector in an economy.

Strategic Vision, Strategy and Implementation

Strategic Vision is the description of the road map answering three questions. Where are we? Where do we want to be? And How do we get there? Crafting the long term strategy that would see Malawi achieve its aspirations of becoming a wealthy nation should be followed by strategy implementation. Failure to turn actions into reality will hurt the dream of becoming a wealthy nation.

Wealthy Nation

Lastly, is the wealthy nation perspective. The issue of moving from poverty to a wealthy nation revolves around the use of all elements presented in the conceptual frame work.

Part II
THE NATION'S WEALTH

CHAPTER 3

Wealth Creation Principles

THE WEALTH OF NATIONS {WN} was published on March 9, 1776 by Adams Smith during the Scottish Enlightenment and the Scottish Agricultural Revolution. It influenced a number of authors and economists, as well as governments and organizations. For example, Alexander Hamilton was influenced in part by *The Wealth of Nations* to write his *Report on Manufactures*, in which he argued against many of Smith's policies. Interestingly, Hamilton based much of this report on the ideas of Jean-Baptiste Colbert, and it was, in part, Colbert's ideas that Smith responded to with *The Wealth of Nations*.

Many other authors were influenced by the book and used it as a starting point in their own work, including Jean-Baptiste Say, David Ricardo, Thomas Malthus and, later, Ludwig von Mises. The Russian national poet Aleksandr Pushkin refers to *The Wealth of Nations* in his 1833 verse-novel Eugene Onegin.

The Wealth of Nations was the product of seventeen years of notes, and observation of conversation among economists of the time concerning economic and societal conditions during the beginning of the Industrial Revolution, and took Smith ten years to produce. The result, An Inquiry to the Wealth of Nations, was a treatise which sought to offer a practical application for reformed economic theory to replace the mercantilist and physiocratic economic theories that were becoming less relevant in the time of industrial progress and innovation. It provided the foundation for new economists, politicians, mathematicians, biologists, and thinkers of all fields to build upon. Irrespective of historical influence, *T*he Wealth of Nations represented a clear shift in the field of economics, comparable to Sir Isaac Newton's Principia Mathematica for physics, Antoine Lavoisier's Traité Élémentaire de Chimie for chemistry, or Charles Darwin's On the Origin of Species for biology.

The Nation's Wealth Per Capita

A nation's wealth is its per capita national product – the amount that the average person actually produces. For any given mix of natural resources that a country might possess, the size of this product will depend on the proportion of the population who are in productive work. But it also depends, much more importantly, on the skill and efficiency with which this productive labour is employed. At the time, this idea was a huge innovation. The prevailing wisdom was that wealth consisted in money – in precious metals like gold and silver. Smith insists that real wealth is in fact what money buys – namely, the 'annual produce of the land and labour of the society'. It is what we know today as gross national product or GNP, and is used as the measure of different countries' prosperity.

Specialisation and Productivity

The key to economic efficiency is specialisation – the division of labour. Take even the trifling manufacture of pin making, for example. Most of us would be hard pressed to make even one pin in a day, even if the metal were already mined and smelted for us. We could certainly not make twenty. And yet ten people in a pin factory can make 48,000 pins a day. That is because they each specialise in different parts of the operation. One draws out the wire, another straightens it, a third cuts it, a fourth points it, a fifth grinds the top to receive the head. Making and applying the head require further specialist operations; whitening the pins and packaging them still more. Specialisation has made the process thousands of times more productive.

This enormous gain in productivity has led to specialisation being introduced, not just within trades, but between them. Farming, for instance, becomes much more efficient if farmers can spend all their time tending their land, their crops and their livestock, rather than pausing to tool up and make their own household items too. Likewise, ironmongers and furniture-makers can produce far more of these household goods if they do not have to dissipate their effort on growing their own food too.

Even whole countries specialise, exporting the goods they make best and importing the other commodities that they need.

The greatest improvement in the productive power of labour, and the greater part of the skill, dexterity, and judgment with which it is anywhere directed, or applied, seems to have been the effects of the division of labour. Three factors explain the enormous rise in efficiency which specialisation makes possible. First is the increased skill which people gain when they do the same task over and over again. The rapidity with which skilled workers can do a task is sometimes amazing.

Second, less time is wasted in moving from one task to the next. A weaver who cultivates a smallholding has to break off weaving, fetch the farming tools, and walk out to the field. It takes time for people to get in the right frame of mind when they turn from one task to another, and back again.

The importance of such disruptions should not be underestimated. Third, specialisation allows the use of dedicated machinery, which dramatically cuts the time and effort needed in manufactures. Often, workers themselves have invented labour saving devices, while other improvements have come from the machine-makers, who are now a specialist set of trades themselves.

The Division of Labour

The division of labour clearly requires an advanced degree of cooperation between all those who are involved in the manufactures concerned. Indeed, the production of even the simplest object harnesses the cooperation of many thousands of people. A woolen coat, for example, requires the work of shepherds, sorters, carders, dyers, spinners, weavers, and many more. Even the shears needed to cut the wool will have required the work of miners and ironworkers. And the transportation of the wool will have required sailors, shipwrights, and sail-makers. The list is endless. The woolen coat, for example, which covers the day-labourer, as coarse and rough as it may appear, is the produce of the joint.

The Condensed 'Wealth of Nations'

The shepherd, the sorter of the wool, the wool-comber or carder, the dyer, the scribbler, the spinner, the weaver, the fuller, the dresser, with many others, must all join their different arts in order to complete even this homely production. This collaboration of thousands of highly efficient specialists is a very advanced economic system: and it is, in fact, the source of the developed countries' great wealth. It means that things are produced far more efficiently, making them cheaper. Even the poorest members of society thereby gain access to a wide variety of products and services that would be completely unaffordable in the absence of specialization.

The mutual gains from exchange

Specialisation developed out of the natural human tendency to barter and exchange. When we see people who have things that we want, we know that they are unlikely to give them to us out of the goodness of their hearts. But then we might have something which they want, and which we would be prepared to give them in return. It is not from the benevolence of the butcher, the brewer, or the baker, that we expect our dinner, but from their regard to their own interest. We address ourselves, not to their humanity but to their self-love, and never talk to them of our own necessities but of their advantages. And this in fact is how we acquire most of the things we need –through exchange, rather than trying to make everything ourselves.

And the trade has made both of us better off. We have each sacrificed something we value less for something we value more. This is another crucial insight. In Smith's world, like ours, most goods were exchanged for money rather than bartered for other goods. Since money was regarded as wealth, it seemed that only the seller could benefit from the process. It is a notion that led to the creation of a vast web of restrictions on trade, in the attempt to prevent money leaking out of a country, a town, or even a profession. But Smith shows that the benefit of exchange is mutual, so no such restrictions are needed.

These gains from exchange, and our natural willingness to do it, stimulate the division of labour. It is worth us building up a surplus of what we personally make well in order to have something to trade with other people. To take it at its simplest, imagine a primitive society where, through some particular mental or physical talents, one person is better than others at making arrows, or building houses, or dressing skins, or working metal. If, through that specialist skill, they make more of these things than they have personal need for, it gives them something they can exchange with others. So each can then focus on their efficient specialist production, and get the other things they need from exchange with other efficient producers. The smith trades surplus knives for the fletcher's surplus arrows, the tanner trades clothing for the builder's shelter. Each ends up with the mix of things they want, all of them expertly and efficiently produced.

Production Costs and Market prices

The wages and profits in any production process tend to an average rate that depends on the market. When the price of a commodity exactly matches the cost (rent, profit, and wages) of producing it and bringing it to market, we might call it the natural price.14 If it sells at more than that, the seller makes a profit. If it sells at less, the seller makes a loss.

CHAPTER 4

The Creation of Wealth and Economic Growth

Production

Production refers to the conversion of inputs, the factors of production, into desired output. An economy-wide production function is often written as follows:

$$X^* = f(L, K, M)$$

where X^* is an aggregate measure of goods and services produced (output) in a given economy.

- **L** represents the quantity and ability of labor input available to the production process.
- **K** represents capital, machinery, transportation equipment, and infrastructure.
- **M** represents the availability of natural resources and materials for production

A positive relationship exists among these inputs and the output such that greater availability of any of these factors will lead to a greater potential for producing output. The functional relationship (f) represents a certain level of technology and know how that presently exists for conversion of these inputs into output such that any technological improvements can also lead to the production of greater levels of output.

Gross Domestic Product

Many economists say that Gross Domestic Product (GDP) **is** the broadest quantitative measure of a nation's total economic activity. More specifically, GDP represents the monetary value of all goods and services produced within a nation's geographic borders over a specified period of time.

The value of a country's overall output of goods and services (typically during one fiscal year) at market prices, excluding net income from abroad. Gross Domestic Product (GDP) can be estimated in three ways which, in theory, should yield identical figures.

The value of a country's overall output of goods and services (typically during one fiscal year) at market prices, excluding net income from abroad. Figure 4.1 below illustrates the circular floor of GDP.

THE CIRCULAR FLOW

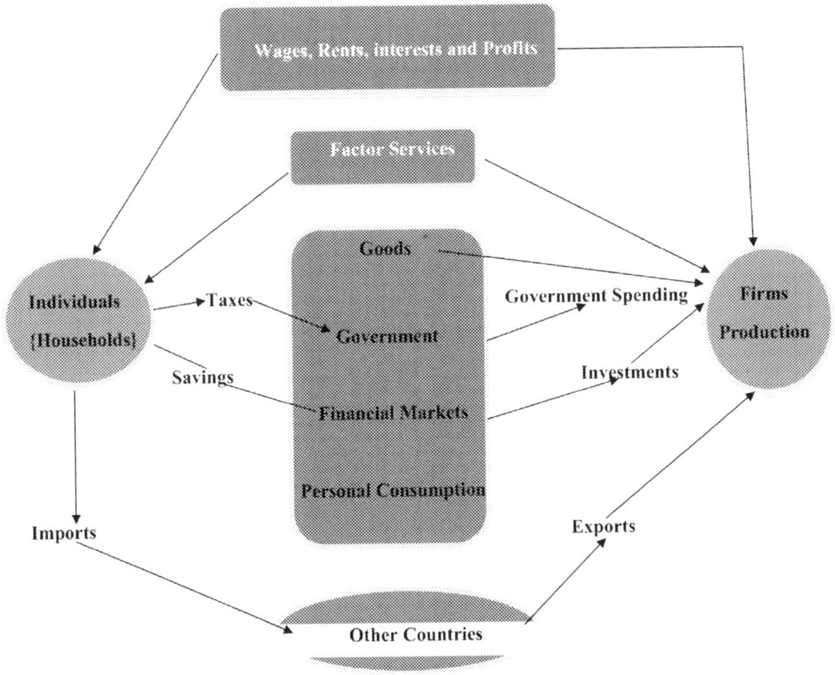

Figure 4:1 The Circular Flow of Gross Domestic Product

Source: Ngwira {2012}

Gross Domestic Product (GDP) can be estimated in three ways which, in theory, should yield identical figures. They are:

1. Expenditure basis: how much money was spent,
2. Output basis: how many goods and services were sold, and
3. Income basis: how much income (profit) was earned.

The equation used to calculate GDP is as follows:

GDP = Consumption + Government Expenditures + Investment + Exports - Imports

The components used to calculate GDP include:

Consumption:

- Durable goods (items expected to last more than three years)
- Nondurable goods (food and clothing)
  - **The green belt initiative**
  I take the green belt initiative as a recreation of wealth policy. Once this is implemented the country would increase production and productivity. This is key to agro processing as the agricultural sector would provide raw material for the industry. As we all know Malawi is an agro based economy and it will remain so for years to come. Once an investment is made in agriculture sector and resources used as intended it will contribute significantly both on backward and forward linkages in all economic fronts. We all know that once food is available in Malawi the inflation rate goes down and we all know the ripple effects. The strategic move here is to deliberately allocate resources to the initiative with complete commitment to see its results. The challenges the country has faced is procrastination of implementation of all the good policies the country has produced.

- Services

Government Expenditures:

- Defense
- Roads
- Schools

Investment Spending:

- Nonresidential (spending on plants and equipment), Residential (single-family and multi-family homes)
- Business inventories

Net Exports:

- Exports are added to GDP
- Imports are deducted from GDP

Why it Matters

When GDP declines for two consecutive quarters or more, by definition the economy is in a recession. Meanwhile, when GDP grows too quickly and fears of inflation arise, the Reserve Bank or Central Bank often attempts to stimulate the economy by raising interest rates.

CHAPTER 5

Wealth Creation Model

IN HIS RESEARCH, Ngwira {2012} designed wealth creation model {WCM} for application. The model highlights four building pillars or blocks that would help see Malawi transform from poverty to a wealth nation. Such pillars are as follows:

(a). Tuning
(b). Adaptation
(c). Reorientation
(d). Re-creation

The four pillars on WCM are shown in Figure 1, below.

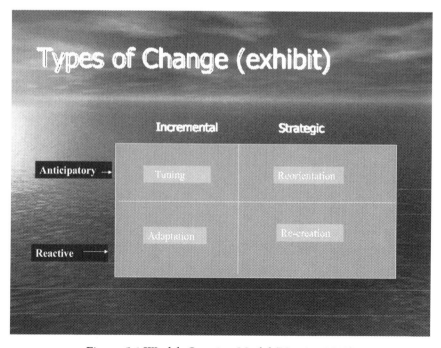

Figure 5:1 Wealth Creation Model {Ngwira 2012}

Details about the four pillars of wealth creation are as follows:

Tuning

Incremental change made in anticipation of future events. This is mainly designed to increase efficiency and not to respond to an immediate problem

Adaptation

Incremental change made in response to external events (for exsmple change in market needs, technology).

Reorientation

Strategic change made on the basis of anticipated external events that may need change. The changes happen through fundamental redirection of the organization with emphasis on continuity of the values of the past. This type of change is referred to as frame-bending change because it does not attempt to sharply break away from the existing organizational frame even though the change could be a major one.

Re-creation

Strategic change dictated by external events that usually threaten the existence of the organization and thus demand radical departure from the past. Change in leadership, values, culture, etc. take place in this kind of change.

Building Wealth

We can create personal, business and state wealth. It's possible to meet our financial goals. By choosing to budget, save and invest, we can be able to manage our operations, investment and economic growth. Building wealth requires having the right information, planning and making good choices.

The first thing to understand wealth is to understand the meaning of **assets**, **liabilities** and **net worth.** They make up this very important formula: **Assets – Liabilities = Net Worth.** *Net worth* is the difference between your assets and liabilities. This means that our wealth as a country our net worth is our wealth.

To build our wealth there is need to seriously think of setting long term financial goals not just for five years but for a longer period such as 50 years. It goes without saying that *If we make a good income each year and spend it all, we will not get wealthier but we will just be living high.*

The next step in building our wealth is to inculcate a culture of saving and investing. For the sake of our discussion investment is the science of money making money. This means as a nation we need to deliberately establish assets which will generate enough cash flow to finance our national development agenda activities. We cannot talk about building wealth without thinking on how we could take control of debt. Remember the definition of net worth (wealth)?

Assets – Liabilities = Net Worth

Liabilities are our debts. Debt reduces net worth. Plus, the interest we pay on debt, debt, is money that cannot be saved or invested—it's just gone. In financial management we look at debt/equity ratio when considering how much debt we should be able to acquisition. Therefore it is important not to borrow more than 50 percent of our equity because there might be more lines of expenditure that will require money apart from money for paying the debt.

Need to fight and reduce Corruption

White collar crime, fraud, false accounting, cheating, extortion and theft are very often facilitated by corruption. The Anti-Corruption Bureau was set due to realization that there is corruption in Malawi and that there is need to arrest corruption which is threatening democracy in the country. It is a known fact that the ACB was established in December 1995 under the Corrupt Practices Act but became operational in 1998 with a mandate to take measures to guarantee accountability, transparency, personal integrity and financial probity in accordance with the constitution of Malawi with a view to act currently and address only bribery or gratification as corruption.

So what is corruption? According to Corrupt Practices Act (1995) corruption is the giving (or offering) and acceptance (or attempting to accept) an advantage as an inducement or reward for doing or not doing an act which amounts to abusing one's official position. This means that two people are involved, the giver and the taker. Thus, both the giver and the taker commit an offence under the Corrupt Practices Act (1995). In this definition, corruption has two elements:

First, the involvement of two or more people in the act of giving (offering, promising). Second, the act of receiving (soliciting, accepting) an advantage as a reward or inducement for a person to do or not to do an act for his own personal benefit. On the other hand many business commentators say that there are two universally accepted levels of corrupt practices: grand corruption and petite corruption. Grand corruption might be multi-sector; involving huge amounts of resources and personnel and usually has international dimensions.

The smuggling of endangered species (ivory), registration of stolen vehicles, issuing of counterfeit legal documents are examples. Thus crime syndicates are established to systematically deprive public or private bodies of legitimate resources. In the recent times legitimate international organizations and businesses are involved in grand corruption to obtain lucrative contracts. Petite corruption usually involves less people, (the giver and taker) and is mostly done in secret.

From the foregoing explanation it shows that people are entangled in corruption for either need or greed. But these have to have other factors such as opportunity in the environment for the crime to take place. The resources involved in the transaction are relatively small. For example, a corrupt traffic officer soliciting a bribe from a minibus conductor, or a clinical officer who is paid "speedy money" to dispense medical drugs quickly are some examples. Thus, people who do not take leave, employees who are over familiar with clients, employees who are sociable with people not of their social standing, frequently breach of company rules and policies and lastly people who live above their means.

According to Corrupt Practices Act (1995) ACB has three statutory functions. First, the investigation and prosecution. In this function, the Bureau investigates and prosecute any public officer or any other person for an offense as defined in Part IV of the Act. In addition, the Bureau can also investigate the conduct of any public officer which is conductive or connected to corruption. Second, civic education. To this effect the Bureau has a statutory responsibility to disseminate information on the evil and dangerous effects of corruption on society and enlist and foster public support in the fight against corruption.

The Bureau does this by producing radio programmes, dramas and plays; erecting "bill boards" in strategic places; sending every Public Officer a "Notice" telling him/her of their duties and responsibilities; produce an ACB Newsletter; hold regular meeting with civic and religious leaders, NGOs and other law enforcement institutions, providing suggestion boxes in strategic places; maintaining close cooperation with government leaders, religious organizations and politicians; holding public meetings and conduct educational tours in rural areas, especially with Traditional Authorities; organizing workshops and seminars for stakeholders; holding regular press briefs and issue press releases; participating in public debates and utilizing the mass media effectively When the above activities take place they result in proper public awareness of the Bureau's functions; good quality reports being made to the bureau; enhanced public support for the Bureau; good relations other agencies and sharing of information and intelligence.

Lastly, corruption prevention. On this the Bureau has a statutory function to: examine the procedures and practices of public and private bodies to identify areas which are prone to corruption; secure the revision of methods of work or procedures which are prone to corruption; and advise public and private bodies on how to prevent corruption. According to Corrupt Practices Act (1995) the Bureau does this by working with clients to review methods and systems of work in order to minimize or eradicate corruption opportunities, introducing new methods and systems in client institutions, conduct "managerial accountability and transparency" workshops to foster improved accountability, maintaining close contact with client organizations in order to monitor and ensure implementation of new ideas and procedural changes, assist in framing codes of conduct for public officer which will include morality, conflict of interest, monitoring declarations of assets and liabilities regularly and study the public procurement process.

Aforementioned activities result in: a reduction in the occurrence of corruption and an increase in public revenue; the efficient delivery of goods, services and works in client institutions; an improvement in the conduct of public officers; an improvement in the public procurement process; better public image for Malawi; more support for government developmental plans; and less risk of public disorder.

Causes of Corruption

People become corrupt because of lack of ethical standards or lack of codes of conduct that prompt people to act with integrity. Thus, competition for insufficient goods and services has also resulted in some people engaging in corruption to access the few goods and services. Other causes of corruption include extreme poverty, high cost of living, greed and dishonesty where even the rich engage in corruption.

According to ACB data bank (2008) opportunities for corruption exist if rules and regulations are outdated or cannot be reinforced because of insufficient manpower. For example, the immigration office in Lilongwe looks overwhelmed with work because most of the time there either two or three officers or sometimes none at all, serving full house of customers. This could result in people offering money to the few officers in order to get their application for passports processed quickly.

Effects of corruption

Corruption if not arrested will be prone to bring the following effects; uneven playing field; hardworking spirit will be eroded resulting in a decline in efficiency and productivity; the cost of running the organization usually goes up making the organization inefficient; money is usually targeted at services that do not benefit the organization; retarded development due to negative impact on organizational efficiency;

Human rights and democracy are negatively affected, reduces quality of services, reduces morale of staff through intimidation and coercion; creates power bases that undermine authority of superiors; creates friction among staff; the general public loses confidence in state structures; reduction of resources going into the government reserves; leads to distortion of development trends; causes injustice; causes deliberate delays in the system for "speedy money" to be paid; expenditure controls undermined leading to budget deficit.

The Government does not collect enough revenue for development projects; poor quality of goods and services are supplied causing the loss of precious resources through frequent replacements; corrodes the values and ethics that govern the business process; poor business image; increase in prices of goods and services; reduces creativity, innovation and reform; can destroy the authority structure and management systems caused by juniors disrespecting their seniors and withdrawal of donor aid.

Factors that lead to corruption

Many writers say corruption is evil and must not be accepted in society. As such there is need to be equipped with factors that lead to corruption. Chinseu (2005) notes the following factors that lead to corruption; regionalism; nepotism; poverty; greed; political patronage; inequalities in staff treatment; high employment; rigid decision making; narrow promotional structures; excessive procedures; monopoly of authority and decision making powers; lack of effective legislation, rules and regulations and that control employee behavior; absence of mechanisms to detect and control conflict of interest; employees not loyal to the organization or objectives; lack of transparency in procurement and tendering of contracts or goods and services; and higher demand for goods and services in relationship to a small supply base promotes unhealthy and excessive competition for limited resources.

Remedies for reducing corruption

Corrupt Practices Act (1995) suggests the following remedies for reducing corruption; codes of conduct to be encouraged; remove unnecessary procedures; encourage media involvement in exposing the corrupt; encourage the dissemination of knowledge on government procedures and processes; stringent enforcement of established legislation against corruption; encourage whistle blowers; encouraging managerial accountability by supervisors on all business decisions made by subordinates.

Part III
STRATEGIC APPROACHES FOR BECOMING A WEALTHY NATION

CHAPTER 6

Strategic Approaches from Free Market to Mixed Economy

ECONOMIC SYSTEMS ALL OVER THE WORLD are three: Command, free market and mixed systems. Case, Fair and Oster {2009} explain more on the aforementioned economic systems: First the command system is also known as socialism or communism. In that system, government owns most property resources and economic decision making occurs through a central economic plan. A central planning board appointed by the government makes nearly all the major decisions concerning the use of resources, the composition and distribution of output and the organization of production. Second, the polar alternative to the command system is the market system.

The system is characterized by private ownership of resources and the use of markets and prices to coordinate and direct economic activity. Lastly, mixed economies allow many more freedoms than command and free market economies, such as the freedom to possess the means of production; to participate in managerial decisions; to buy, sell, fire, and hire as needed; and for employees to organize and protest peacefully. Simply put a mixed economy is an economy in which there are elements of both public and private features.

Free Market System

Brue and Mc Connell 2008 says a free market is a system in which the prices for goods and services are determined by the open market and consumers, in which the laws and forces of supply and demand are free from any intervention by a government, price-setting monopoly, or other authority. This means that free market refers to an economy where the government imposes few or no restrictions and regulations on buyers and sellers. In a free market, participants determine what products are produced, how, when and where they are made, to whom they are offered, and at what price—all based on supply and demand {Brue and Mc Connell 2008}.

For countries that favour a free market economy it has the following advantage: *it* promotes the production and sale of goods and services, with little to no control or involvement from any central government agency; A free market economy is driven by individual innovation and the notion that hard work and ingenuity will be rewarded by success. All businesses exist to make a profit.

Therefore, in the free market system, a successful business makes a consistent profit in a field of competitors. The concept of competition is an important component of a free market system. Additionally, it also allows for individuals to innovate.

Competition in the marketplace provides the best possible product to the customer at the best price. When a new product is invented, it usually starts out at a high price, once it is in the market for a period of time, and other companies begin to copy it, the price goes down as new, similar products emerge. In a competitive market, the poor versions of the product or the overpriced will be pushed out of the market because consumers will reject them. The free market system determines the winners and losers in each industry based on the demands of the customer, whether industrial, business customers, or consumers, people who buy for personal use.

However, disadvantages are created from some of the advantages. Profit motive drives businesses, but can create dangers. Poor working conditions and unethical decisions can be made as entrepreneurs seek higher profits. Secondly, free markets can lead to market crashes as we saw in the great depression and the economic downturn in the early 2000's. Unemployment can lead to devastation of families. These advantages lead to economic growth and expansion during the business cycle. However, during times of crashes and downturns, government regulation usually occurs to spur expansion again.

The key feature of a free market economy is that market forces dictate what is produced, in what quantities, at what price, and for which consumers. Resources are privately owned by individuals and companies. Profit and return on investment are the main drivers of businesses. History has shown that free market economies perform substantially better than government-run economies. They have proven to be more responsive to customer needs, and create a wider variety of products than alternative economic approaches. Intense competition pressures firms to produce ever-better goods and services at lower cost and more efficiently.

Mixed Economy

According to {Nickels and Hugh 2005} a *mixed economic* system is an *economic* system that features characteristics of both capitalism and socialism. A *mixed economic* system allows a level of private economic freedom in the use of capital, but also allows for governments to interfere in economic activities in order to achieve social aims. Mixed economies have a high level of state participation and spending, leading to tax-funded libraries, schools, hospitals, roads, utilities, legal assistance, welfare, and social security. Various restrictions on business are made for the greater good, such as environmental regulation, labor regulation, antitrust and intellectual property laws. The ideal combination of these freedoms and restrictions is meant to ensure the maximum standard of living for the population as a whole.

Just as the free market economy the mixed economy also has advantages: a mixed economy permits private participation in production, which in return allows healthy competition that can result in profit. It also contributes to public ownership in manufacturing, which can address social welfare needs; State provides the essential services; Private sector encouraged for profits; Competition keeps prices low; there are consumer choices or alternatives and inefficient business behavior controlled. However, there also disadvantages of a mixed economy: heavy taxes reduce incentives to work hard or make profits less efficient and excessive control over business activity can add costs and discourage enterprise.

Malawi Needs a Mixed Economic System

From the discussion above Malawi needs move from free market economy and adopt a mixed economic system. This system will allow all players such as individuals or households, firms or companies and the state to take part in the running of the economy. This is one of the many solutions that Malawi needs to come out of poverty and become a wealth nation.

CHAPTER 7

From Public Administration to the New Public Management

The Public Administration

THE PUBLIC SERVICE OR BUREAUCRACY is an instrument of the state which implements government policy. This is public administration, a sector that takes charge of the planning and implementation of national development programs in the country. The traditional public sector or bureaucracy, as set of institutions, rules and regulations and as haven for rationality, has been generally criticized for corruption, patriomonialism, wastefulness, inefficiency and ineffectiveness for various reasons. One main cause, it is argued, of these misadministration is growing size of government, a thing, which makes its public sector or bureaucratic structures wasteful, less accountable, remote, unresponsive and inefficient.

These charges have precipitated ideologically conservative public sector reforms aimed at withdrawing the role of the state from the economy and polity and instead introduce private ownership and free market economics as neo-liberal alternatives to the stalled development process. These reforms were and some are being implemented through large scale privatization of national industries, liberalization of the economy and politics that aims at reducing the size of the public sector or bureaucracy to enhance its efficiency, accountability and responsiveness to needs.

The "simple nostrum" in these reforms is that government will function better if it operates as though it were in the private sector. The focus of this "New Public Management" is that government must be result-oriented. This is different from the traditional approach that looks at the public sector as an administrative instrument. Rather merely policy and development processes with the main objective of achieving specified objectives against which its performance is judged.

The other brand of bureaucratic reforms is that of people's empowerment to enable them participate in government activities and influence public policy processes and development. These public sector reforms are not entirely successful in developing countries. Whereas empowerment implies equity among citizens in the process of allocating public resources, in developing countries family, religious and other social benchmarks are regarded as appropriate ways of allocating scarce resources. The function of the free market depends on the capacity and willingness to measure quality and performance but this is lacking in most public services in developing countries.

Liberalization that encourages privatization, deregulation and commodification of public services in developing countries has the potential of opening up government to more corruption and the politicization of the civil service as different sections scramble for the new cherry-pickings. In the name of greater efficiency public services have been contracted out, development projects franchised to private companies; state spending slashed; user charges for basic services introduced or increased; and markets deregulated In the process power and wealth have become increasingly concentrated and the ability of nation states to protect the public interest has been undermined.

The chief of nation states to protect the public interest has been undermined. The chief beneficiaries have been transnational corporations, capitalists and the local elite. The public sector is a multiplex gamut seen as a social, political and cultural institution encompassing through its specialized functions, the sociology, the economy, the polity and the history of a nation.

The New Public Management

The New Public Sector Management is an attempt to turn around the public sector from being traditional and routine administrative processes catering for the subjects and citizens to a scientific, results oriented, performance based and market friendly business strategically postured to serve the needs of customers and citizens alike.

The background to all this that the public sector has recently reeled under the neo-liberal blitz that argues for values of a results-oriented, performance based, efficient and highly productive sizeable public sector. This is a typical of a private sector driven economy and development strategy. It entails an attack on the traditional state bureaucracy or public sector, which it seeks to modify and reform along the free market economics philosophy.

It prescribes free market economics; and implies the use of the cost-benefit-analysis (CBA), the Pareto Optimally and the Kaldor Criterion (adapted from Howlett M. & Ramesh M. 1995:30). As to what extent have these measures been successful remains to be seen. The CBA is essentially a technique for making the government replicate market decision-making as closely as possible for the purpose of allocating resources.

In this attempt, the criterion of Pareto Optimality principle has however not been that successful in transforming the public sector because all government replicate market decision-making at least one person better off without worsening the situation of any other person. The Pareto Optimality principle has however not been that successful in transforming the public sector because all government actions make some better off at the expense of others.

Because of such problems inherent in the nature of government and the public sector, the Kaldor criterion, which requires that only policy alternatives maximizing net benefits over cost be chosen. Under this criterion, a policy can be chosen even if some lose as long as the total gains are higher than sum of losses Of central concern here is the macro-economic environment of the public sector.

Fiscal and monetary policy is certainly an alpha and omega in this debate. The bloated, inefficient and corrupt public sector has been seen as a source of high public expenditure and fiscal indiscipline. With these instruments, governments have since public sector reforms been urged to move towards stimulating productivity and income generation rather than managing consumption and public expenditure.

CHAPTER 8

Improving the Machinery of Government

THE STRUCTURE OF GOVERNMENT and allocation of functions to Departments and Ministries are often collectively referred to as "machinery of government". International practice provides a range of approaches: mandates, responsibilities and accountabilities should be clearly allocated avoiding duplication and overlaps; the structure should be simple and robust. Principles on which the structure is based should be clear to all sets of stakeholders; the structure should provide Ministers with an appropriate span of control; the structure should promote a strong client orientation, and be based on a rough delineation between policy formulation and implementation responsibilities; the structure should provide for maximum possible decentralization of service delivery responsibilities to regions and local government.

A constitution establishes the regulatory framework for political activity and the governance process in a country. One of the things it does is to establish organs of government, define their functions and specify their powers for the discharge of these functions. Experience from all over the world and from time immemorial has taught that three particular organs of government are the most basic. These are: (a) the Executive (b) the Legislature and (c) the Judiciary

These organs correspond to the vital and most basic governance functions namely: The conduct of policy administration; the making or repealing or amendment of governing laws and although all constitutions will provide for the three organs, their functions and powers, the constitutions of different countries thereafter take a different approaches, as some may go further and provide for additional governance – related organs.

Supporting economic development priorities – jobs, innovation and competitiveness

There is need to deliberately create jobs through innovation and competitiveness and bring many of the key levers and functions that drive economic development such as regional development and small business, together with key services to sectors such as agriculture, the creative industries, resources and tourism.

The consolidation of functions could be intended for facilitating better communication, coordination and alignment in relation to policy-making, service delivery and investment into the various industry sectors.

Fragmentation

This is the breaking up of the traditional organizations of the welfare of states. For example, splitting local government into more independent units, with schools running themselves and social services divided into specifies and providers. When combined together with privatization and contracting-out this leads even more to the development of networks of suppliers with centrally controlled funding, rather than to the traditional organization bureaucracies.

Machines, Brains and Politics

Machines are the type of organizational structures (public sector organizations) with hierarchical systems of planning and controlling based on notion of single "rationality" which could be imposed on the organization from the top management. It involves establishment of single chains of command with clear accountabilities and lines of communication usually represented on the organizational charts.

Brains are public sector organizations that can capture and process information and thus be more responsive to their environment. The brains can be 'messy' structures than machines because learning and information processing does not only occur at the top of the organization. However, the general pattern has been to attach a research and intelligence unit to the machine. This can have as much or little impact as the machine wishes.

Politics are the public sector organizations behaving as political systems,.i.e. focusing on the power relationships within them in this case, there is a tendency to interpret the activities of managers and workers as attempts to gain power. In short, politics look at people working in public sector organizations as trying to maximize their own income and satisfaction.

CHAPTER 9

Enhancing the Private Sector through Government Support

WE CANNOT TALK ABOUT enhancing the private sector through government support without thinking of public private partnerships. As pointed out earlier the private sector is the engine of economic growth. From observation our private sector is very weak since it is characterized by slow down of business transactions to the extent that some firms are closing. Many companies have also seen the retrenchment of their staff at all levels. Additionally, there has also been low purchasing power due to continued depression of kwacha, low tax collections, higher levels of gearing by Government, high inflation and interest rates that have contributed to the down fall of many businesses. To address some of these flaws comes the need to engage the public private partnership.

Models for enhance the private sector

Formulating a strategy for continuous improvement is critical. This means there is need to redesign the government to improve the way of doing business by flattening and encouraging cross-functional teams, as well as combining ministries and departments. The following models could be considered:

- **The planning model** {which includes: developing the need for change, establishing relationships, clarifying the problem, examining alternatives, implementing the change, stabilizing the change}
- **Problem solving model** (includes: problem awareness and identification, information gathering, generating solutions, decision, implementation and review)

- **Need-satisfaction model** (includes: need identification, initial diagnosis, action)
- **Growth model** (starting from the infant stage to maturity)
- **Ice model** (unfreezing, moving to the new state and refreezing)
- **Transition model** (diagnosis, defining the end state, defining the transition state, strategizing, evaluating and stabilizing)
- **Primary activity model** (generating information, allowing free and informed choice, and fostering internal commitment)

CHAPTER 10

Financing the Public or Private Sector: Equity or Debt?

IN FINANCIAL REPORTING, we normally deal with financial statements that an organization's accounting system produces including the profit and loss account also commonly called Income Statement, the balance sheet also called statement of financial position and cash flow statements. The income statement presents the financial performance, the statement of financial position also called balance sheet presents the financial position while cash flow represents the financial adaptability. Out of the three financial statements the balance sheet or statement of financial position which represents assets, capital and liabilities shows how an entity is financed.

Show me the Money

Finding the funds to finance activities is usually one of the most challenging things the nation will face. However the good news is that money is available. The bad news is that it is sometimes harder to secure than you may anticipate. But look around. Every country that is prospering began as someone's dream and, some-how, the leaders of that country found the wisdom to open their doors to financial prosperity and become a wealth nation. If they did, so we can.

Money and the Wealth

The very first thing required is to accurately estimate the amount of money we need from the nation's financial budget. Taking a cold, hard look at our wealth requirements will help us know success better. Once we know how much wealth we need, it will be incumbent for us to get it. Having a cash crunch from the start is a sure way to go out of business fast. Moreover, a realistic budget will help convince a lender or investor that you understand your business and are worth the risk. The national budget or corporate budget is the first thing we always need to know how much money we will need to run the country in a given financial year and should show clearly how we intend to spend it.

How much wealth do we need?

If we create a strategic plan say for 5 years for a company or 50 years and beyond for the nation, we should have a pretty good idea how much wealth we will need. If you haven't figured it out yet, this section will be of much help. One of the areas we need to become wealth is money. The money we will need can be divided into three categories: one-time costs, working capital, and ongoing costs. One-time costs are things that we will need to spend money on to. The minister of finance or an accountant for a company has a role on this.

Financing the financial deficit of a corporation or a country deals with deciding the capital structure. Capital structure explains how an entity is financed. Entities are either financed either by equity finance or debt finance. These are the main sources of finance. However, each of these has cost of acquisitioning the funds. These are cost of equity and cost of debt or cost of borrowing. The entity pays cost of debt normally this is an interest. Although debt is a way of financing a an entity in many cases the financial institutions such as local banks, world financial institutions such as World Bank {WB} or International Monetary Fund {IMF} do not provide the funds without touched strings.

Since they are two options for financing the country financial deficit: equity or debt the corporation or the nation can decide to obtain the equity funds from taxation or borrow from lenders of finance such as WB or IMF or any other financial institution whether local or international. Similarly the managers of a corporation can get funds either from shareholders as equity funds or borrow from professional investors such as banks.

Therefore in most cases, a nation's or company funds may be viewed as a pool of resource, that is, a combination of different funds with different costs. Under such circumstances it might seem appropriate to use an average cost of capital for investment approval.

From the foregoing we can conclude that public finance deals with services that are financed by taxation. Thus the role of the government in the economy. It is the branch of economics which assesses the government revenue and government expenditure of the public authorities and the adjustment of one or the other to achieve desirable effects and avoid undesirable ones.

Based on the discussion above although any entity can be finance by either equity or debt finance it is important to decide to what extent should a company or nation should borrow. The answer to this lies in the financial deficit the company or nation has in its budget.

On the part of government this is a call to always implement good fiscal policies in which government should reduce borrowing and cut down expenditure. This will provide real financial independence in a long run. This means that government must craft deliberate long term policies beyond five years say 50 years for example that will see the nation move out of debt type of finance. Donor dependency should be completely abandoned in the long term plans. To enhance both private and public sector finance there will be need to consider the following changes:

{a} **Adaptation Change**

Adaptation is change which can be accommodated within the current paradigm and would occur incrementally. It is the most common form of change in organizations.

{b} **Reconstruction**

It is the type of change which may be rapid and could involve a good deal of upheaval in an organization. It could be a turn around situation where there is a need for a major cost cutting programs to deal with a financial decline problem.

{c} Evolution

Evolution is a change in strategy which requires paradigm changes but over time. It may be that managers anticipate the need for transformational change. This can also be viewed from the point of conceiving the country's as learning systems. This will require continually adjusting strategies as the environment changes. This has learnt credence to the idea of learning organizations

{d} Revolution

Revolution is change which requires rapid and major strategic and paradigm change. A major departure from the norm or routine. This occurs in circumstances where the strategy has been bounded by existing paradigm and established ways of doing things in the organization. To the extent that even when environmental and competitive forces require fundamental change the organization has failed to respond. This might have occurred over many years and often a takeover threatens the continued existence of the firm.

The various changes discussed above will need the concept of creation rather than recreation. Malawi needs creation. In this case to create a new and better Malawi these changes: adaptation; reconstruction; evolution and revolution will be critical. Over many years of study on how our country can transform from poverty to become a wealth nation. I have come with analysis in the way in which the structure and imagery of literature have been affected by the complex of ideas and images surrounding the word 'creation.' Traditionally, everything associated with nature, reality, settled order, the way things are, is supposed to go back to the creation, the original divine act of making the world. If the word 'creative' is applied to human activities, the humanly creative is whatever profoundly disturbs our sense of 'the' creation, a reversing or neutralizing of it.

Creating Vibrant Public Sector Reforms

CREATING VIBRANT PUBLIC SECTOR REFORMS requires that the public sector must be performance based, result oriented and should operate as if it wer the private sector. In this move, instead of merely administering public policy, the public sector should manage the economy and development policy. It should generate revenue while mitigating public expenditure on economically unproductive venture to bring stability into the economy. This implies, socially, introducing and managing liberal transformative forces in the management of the economy and the policy beyond routine linear administrative processes and reforms in the state.

Liberalization, Civil Society, the Media and their Impact on the Public Sector

Neo-liberalism demands that the public sector should play a key role in public governance and development processes. The liberalization of economic and political space has therefore given rise to the role of non-governmental organizations (NGOs), civil society, the media and other non-state actors in public governance and development processes. There is no single definition of the civil society, however, that is acceptable to everybody. In fact, there are as many definitions of civil society as there are people.

What is generally agreeable, however, is that civil society is that space, institution, social process and interaction above the individual and yet below the state. Wiseman Chirwa (2002)offers two approaches used when looking at the civil society as an institution and civil society as a process of human interactions. As an institution, civil society is defined as an informal or formal institution whose members are engaged primarily in a complex of activities outside the state structures.

These activities may include economic, social and cultural production, voluntary association and household life, which either preserves or transforms the institution's identity and exert pressure or controls on the state structures. Such activities allow the people outside government or state structures to interact with each other and with those in government and state echelons.

It is because of this role that the media is perceived as part of civil society, which connects people with government. The media exposes to the people what government is doing with the mandate the people gave it and takes information about people feelings, views and attitudes regarding their government to the government. As a process of human interactions, civil society is defined as an organized social life standing between the individual and state. It is the process that connects the individual with the state. A political side of society where entertainment, conflicts and conflict resolutions and negotiations take place; information is passed and values are learnt.

Civil society, in this sense, is more than mere physical place as it encompasses a process of human interactions. Civil society organizations can also be developmental, issue-centered, interest-based and/or just spiritual or religious in nature. Because of this diversity, civil society is seen as providing good ground for the consolidation of a culture of pluralism in many democratic and developmental aspects. The opening up of a civil space implies that the public sector now faces competition from other actors and stakeholders involved in public affairs. It is argued that competition, checks and balances posed by plurality of actors is an incentive for the public sector to move towards tenets of good governance; accountability, efficiency and effectiveness in its activities.

Creating Adjustments

In pursuit of moving from poverty to a wealth state deliberate strategic moves such as to abandon donor dependency in a long term will be a wise decision. This means that there is need to live in the future while in the present. This calls for crafting a clear strategic vision and the mission statement for the nation.

Strategic Approach

Some adjustments that could be made to realize this dream include: careful consideration when, devaluating the currency, Cutting public expenditure, reducing borrowing, deregulating the free market economy and move to a mixed economy in which both public and private sector are all key players, Reduction of the state in economy for example control of banks, increase taxes (or their collection), reform interest rates (to reduce credit., liberalize foreign trade for example lower tariffs and removal of quotas, reduce subsidies – to farmers, on food, transport and energy, more fees for more services, develop marketing systems, attract foreign direct investment (DFI), reduce government expenditure on social services, getting prices right.

Privatization and the Public Sector

Privatization which is the transfer of control and responsibility for state organizations, functions public services and goods from government or the public sector to private agencies and individuals. It is a process mainly aimed at encouraging private sector participation and modifying or discouraging monopolistic tendencies that have proved to be inefficient as instruments of allocating scarce resources. Whereas in the past, the state took full control and responsibility over such functions and entities, with the current wave of privatization the market is the modus operandi of managing such issues.

The withdrawal of the state in managing assets and the economy is done through different modes of privatization. For example, this is achieved either by means of partial or full load-shedding. Load-shedding is a process of denationalization of public enterprising. There are different motives for privatizing state functions, services and/or organizations. These include; the desire to induce efficiency, economic competition, diversification, cut costs and monopoly and enhance productivity in the public sector as it sheds off wasteful burdens of managing loss making operations. Instead, the public sector is pegged on cash budgets, cost sharing and cost-recovery measures

Privatization of profit making entities is encouraged as a way of attracting investments into the economy. However, if for political reasons, the selling of such entities is resisted partial load-shedding may be an option where shares are sold to workers or outsiders to reduce state control. These entities are attractive to the buyer because they are profit making. For example, in its ardent pursuit of capital and profits, the market has greatly undermined social welfare functions performed by the state. This has raised the question as to whether privatization and private sector growth and/or development or the market are indeed the solution to problems facing the state bureaucracy or public sector in the developing world, Africa and elsewhere.

Government through privatization is losing the vehicles of administering discretionary welfare functions, increasing unemployment levels for capitalists maintain few workers so as to maximize profits, losing tools vital for organizing certain critical activities essential for national survival and economic stability, giving away instrument that enable the state to pursue the objective of preventing the concentration of wealth or the means of production and exchange in the hands of few individuals and most importantly losing sources of revenue generation that add to available national capital for financing development projects and welfare programs.

In other words, private control of and participation in the economy requires that these be complimented by tenets of social justice as instruments of poverty alleviation. It is not enough to dismantle and sell off public assets to private capital or simply restructure the public sector through privatization. Others have noted that privatization is more a political act than an economic one. Thus, in the absence of an enterprising local base for privatization, the process of denationalization leads to exporting control of the economy to foreign entities.

Improving Productivity/Performance in the Public Sector

Productivity is here defined as the effective and efficient use of resources to achieve outcomes. It involves the level of present effectiveness and efficiency, and the processes to achieve it. However, although labor is the major resource employed by the public sector, there are almost no checks on how well it is being used. On the other hand, money, another key resource, is subject to checks and controls by the Auditor General and the Ministry of Finance and Development Economic Planning. In the private sector, productivity is measured as the ratio of outputs over inputs. The final outputs (goods and services) are divided by resources used in production such as land, labour and capital to find total factor productivity growth. The public sector produces social goods and services with unique characteristics. These characteristics include the fact that these goods are non-divisive and therefore no discrimination is possible in their distribution

Consequently, it is difficult to price goods and services like police services. These goods are also likely to be consumed at the moment they are produced. Consumption and production occur almost at the same time. Most social goods are produced as services to the public and as such are consumed without much economic transaction taking place.

However, it is still important to measure public sector productivity for assessing its impact on the public and the effectiveness of functional and temporal performance enhancement measures. These include setting benchmarks for performance, accountability, responsiveness to the public, planning and budgetary measures.

Quality is an important measure of performance. Public sector goods and service quality should be seen as first a dimension of competitive strategy where quality of each entity is measured and seen as a determinant of performance against other entities. Secondly, quality as a functional strategy where resource productivity is maximized through coordination and integration of activities and the development of expertise in a functional area. Thirdly, quality as a single organizational strategy. Here, quality is the sole objective of the organization sometimes with little or no thought as to how to achieve it.

The organization may thus produce goods that are technically perfect but with little or no demand for them. Fourthly, quality based on customer (client) orientation strategy where quality is seen in terms of attributes such as comfort, accuracy, promptness, safety, reliability and so on. The dilemma of productivity in the public sector is based on the political emphasis by government agencies to serve clients rather than customers. This defeats the purpose of having quality strategies. However, the New Public Management demands rather than serving citizens who have obligations to the state, the public sector should serve customers who have consumer rights to be protected. Public allocation of resources should reflect efficiency and effectiveness, creative rather than conservative government that strive multiple economic, social and political obstacles so that private, individual and collective actions can be more effective.

Part IV

THE NATURE OF THE PUBLIC SECTOR

CHAPTER 12

Principles and Control of the Public Sector

PIONEERED BY SCHOLARS LIKE MAX WEBER, the public sector or state bureaucracy has become to be generally known as an institution marked by a hierarchy of authority, routine command and formal lines of communication, role specialization, appointment of officers based on merit, permanent tenure of office, structural remuneration, rigid rules and regulation and institutional impersonality. In other words, "it implies inefficiency, rigidity, impersonal rules, unexplained decisions and a host of other forms of maladministration".

Indeed, "despite the connotations, the exact meaning of bureaucracy is simply a formal structure of offices governed by authority and rules. In former communist regimes, the bureaucracy was marked by centralization and party control. In the remaining communist states nonetheless, "functional and personnel overlap of party and state bureaucracy is an enduring feature. In many third world authoritarian regimes, the key characteristics are "the relatively large size and remoteness, corruption and patronage of bureaucracies. "But in all systems the bureaucratic structures exhibit a large degree of independence in practice – no matter how closely they may be controlled by the political elite in theory".

This independence is requisite to the performance of the main function of the bureaucracy that of providing policy leadership to government. Policy implementation at all levels is the major task of bureaucracies. The bureaucracies are also instrumental in drafting delegated legislation which although supervised by parliament gives the executive much freedom of action. In all political systems, political parties, national assemblies and political leaders are the legitimate forces that represent the people not permanent administrators.

It means therefore that public administrators or bureaucrats lack political legitimacy in their quest to serve the national interest. Thus it is the responsibility of legitimate political forces to control the public administrators. The challenge however is to manage and balance the conflict between the need for a democratic and representative government on the one hand and that for an efficient administrative system on the other.

The political controls at the exposure of legitimate political forces over the administrators include recruitment, supply of money, anti-corruption and pro-efficiency legal/judicial mechanism. These controls are sometimes put in place to serve more cryptic purposes. For example, most senior members of the public administration system often share hefty social backgrounds with the political elite. Recruitment in this process depends on social class, prestige and education prevalent in the political main stream. Nevertheless, executive political control of the bureaucracy is never absolute.

The expertise, career specialization, ability to control sources of technical information, division of labour and hierarchical structure of bureaucracies pose obstacles to absolute political control. These values allow the bureaucracy to inspire greater public trust than the politicians in many systems. The values and the ability to stay above over the political competition, like the judiciary, enable the bureaucracy to provide stability, coherence and continuity in the political system needed for development.

Theoretical and Ideological Foundations of Government

Theoretically, government is based on the consent of the governed obtained through a free and fair electoral process or otherwise. By giving their consent to the ruler, the ruled give legitimacy to the authority of the ruler, which make them consequently and politically obliged to obey that authority. This means the ruled have a moral duty to obey the authority of the ruler. That is, the citizens have a duty to obey their government. This duty is an obligation. It is called political obligation.

Political obligation then is the basis of critical citizenship in which the consent of the ruled (citizens) to be governed obliges of critical citizenship in which the consent of the ruled (citizens) to be governed obliges them to obey their ruler (governors). The relationship that binds the ruler and the ruled is one embedded in a social contract in which the ruler and the ruled agree to form government wherein the ruler (as beneficiaries) of the trust. Government is thus viewed as a trust. Political ideologies, on the other hand, form the basis of government as a set of ideas. A political ideology is a system of ideas that provide a framework for people's aspiration to set forth an ideal society wherein human beings would achieve their ultimate potential. That is to say, political ideologies form the basis, which provides people with a distinct choice of what type of government they want to prevail in their society.

Political ideologies, in this sense, can either be descriptive (to explain how humans do live) or prescriptive (to explain how humans ought to live); or explaining and reforming existing conditions for people's welfare (see Ingersoll & Matthews 1991 p5). Thus, we find liberal or conservative ideologies, socialist, communist, capitalists sets of ideas and other ideological strands that form the ideals around which people strive to govern themselves. This, however, is closely related to different attitudes towards the economy and, in particular, the ownership of wealth.

Communists, on the far left, for example, believe in a planned economy, socialists and modern liberals believe in a mixed economy and government regulation, right wing conservatives believe in free market capitalism and private property. As a science of ideas, an ideology also has a pejorative meaning, implying dogmatic, doctrinaire, extreme or simply false.... it is a set of ideas which men posit, explain and justify the ends and means of organized social action, irrespective of whether such action aims to preserve, amend, uproot or rebuild a given social order...ideologies can defend and uphold a particular social order, preventing change from occurring, as in the case of conservatism.

In contrast, liberalism and social democracy have proclaimed the need for reform and social change. Other ideologies, such as communism, fascism and anarchism, have advocated revolution, the overthrow and replacement of the social order itself (Heywood 1992 p.6-7) (own emphasis).

Constitutional and Legal Foundations of Government

Constitutional rules provide ultimate benchmarks for powers of government. These rules are the basis upon which government authority and action is based. The constitution, argues Sunkin (1997: 168-9), provides a framework within which regulatory schemes and standards are set and disputes mediated. However, the extent to which government has legal capacity to intervene in social and economic activity is politically contentious.

Of course, constitutions are also based on ideological principles. For example, rightists (conservatives) believe that government intervenes too much in public affairs and they call for the rolling back of frontiers of the state and view deregulation as necessary precondition for economic growth. They see free markets as better way of satisfying needs than collective political decision-making. For the leftists, however, government action to regulate the operations of the free market and fill its gaps is necessary precondition for economic growth. They see free markets as a better way of satisfying needs than collective political decision-making.

For the leftists, however, government action to regulate the operations of the free market and fill its gaps is necessary and interventions in the form of providing social welfare benefits are essential for a just and fair society. Thus countries have liberal or conservative constitutions and other forms, which give power to government officials and determine government intervention in public affairs. The hallmark is that without proper legal underpinnings for their actions, government officials are powerless to regulate, inspect, raise money by taxation, license, impose new criminal sanctions and so on.

In fact, if they attempt to do without legal authority, their action may be invalid. Governments, then, derive their constitutional and legal authority from the constitution, Acts of Parliament, delegated legislation made by ministers, the executive prerogative, international treaties of member states and other sources.

Principles and Powers of Government Limited Government

In its simplest sense, limited government means that government ministers and officials, like anybody else, ought to comply with particular legal rules contained in legislation and common law. Or, that there ought to be a constitutional ethic regarding legality of government acts, which impose limitations on the institutions of government in the interests of liberty. Liberty is important because it means the spaces within which an individual interacts with fellow individuals and civil societies inside and outside government structures on an equal basis in politics, in the economy, within the social arena, for cultural production and exchange, intellectual development and other activities. Governments are obliged to guarantee this space to all their citizens equally. The principle of limited government, therefore, limits government in order to ensure that these spaces are not trespassed arbitrarily by its acts.

CHAPTER 13

Structure of the Public Sector and Government

THIS IS BASICALLY COMPOSED OF THE CABINET AND THE PUBLIC SECTOR. It is the executive branch of government headed by the head of government and the state – for example the president in Malawi. Its main function is to initiate and execute policy and law. Increasingly, the executive has taken up the lawmaking function as well. In presidential systems, for example, where the president is elected directly by the people, the executive has a representative function too.

The policy and lawmaking process however cuts across the legislature, which gives the policy legal authority and the judiciary, which interprets the law and oversees the implementation of policy terms in line with the law and the constitution. The executive has another function – that of appointing the public sector or bureaucracy. Each elected executive comes with its own cadre of bureaus and, sometimes, it also maintains bureaucratic elements of the previous regime.

Ideally, the powers and influence of the executive on the bureaucracy need to go beyond appointing and dismissing the bureau; the executive must continuously affect the behavior of those it has appointed. Caution is often taken during such appointments not to disregard electoral issues, party balance of power and the danger of leaving outside government prominent rivals who could become a centre for discontent (Ball & Peters op.cit. p.211).

Thus, stability of the executives derives from the party, loyal interest groups, the military and other influential groups in society. However, the permanence, independence, expertise, specialized information and knowledge of the bureaucracy provide checks to the influence of the executive, which is usually so ubiquitous among the ministers.

The relative independence of the bureaucracy from the executive, unlike the cabinet, enhances separation of powers, checks and balances in government. Unlike the legislature and the judiciar. Former US president, Woodraw Wilson, once argued that one the greatest of the president's powers... (is) his control which is very absolute, of the foreign relations of the nation (cited in Ball and Peters op cit. p.210). Of course, in matters of international law, the judiciary plays a pivotal role for a country but still under the sanctions of the executive.

It is assumed that an elected executive carries the general will of the nation. This function is crucial perhaps because it embodies the conscience of the nation and sovereignty of the state. The nature and power of the political executives differ from one political system to the other. In some parliamentary systems like Britain, there are differences between the political head of government and the ceremonial head of state; the Prime Minister, Chancellor, President and the King or Queen.

In presidential systems like the United States, the roles are fused in one person. That is to say, the executive roles of the prime minister and the ceremonial functions of the Queen are deposited in the presidency. In liberal democracies like Malawi, political executives may be divided into two types – prime ministerial and presidential systems or a hybrid thereof – although there are expectations.

In a presidential system, the people elect the president separately from the assembly and he has powers to form government. For example, in America, there are separations of powers among the presidency, the Supreme Court, the congress and senate. Of course overlaps are there where the president has power to appoint senior civil servants such as court judges.

In this system, there is an emphasis on separation of powers. The president is accountable to the people. In a parliamentary system, the Prime Minister is elected to parliament just like any other Member of Parliament. However, his party must obtain a majority in the assembly so that he forms a government after being ceremoniously appointed by the Queen, King or President.

In actual sense, the electorate through the party elects the Prime Minister. In this system, the government is usually chosen from among the elected members in the assembly. Thus, the cabinet is responsible to the assembly, which elects it. It (cabinet) must explain and defend its policies in the assembly.

If the assembly withdraws its support of the cabinet, the prime minister and his entire cabinet resign en masse or advise the president, Queen or King to dissolve parliament in order to seek fresh support and mandate through general elections. But the distribution of the powers of the chief executives is not a simple matter. It is important to note, comment Ball and Peters, that constitutional frameworks often hide more than they show about the distribution of political power with regard to chief executives.

The realities are that political executives are rarely representative as they reflect the power of the dominant social class in society. This social class uses different means at its disposal to attain power. In socialist regimes, the dominant class maneuvers through the single party, which also controls the bureaucracy to power.

In liberal democracies, competitive intra-party and inter-party elections are the means of gaining or retaining constitutional power. There are also extra-constitutional means attaining executive power such as coups, civil wars and an imposition by foreign forces. With the advent of regionalism, executive power can also be attained through selection of the executive by national governments such as the European Commission.

Part V
THE NATURE OF THE PRIVATE SECTOR

CHAPTER 14

Principles of the Private Sector

THE SHORTAGE OF INFRASTRUCTURE in developing countries is an important obstacle to meeting populations' needs, to enterprise development and to achieving the goals of the Millennium Declaration. Many countries face the double challenge of growing demand and ageing physical assets in large parts of their infrastructure sectors, which could become an obstacle to sustained growth. In many countries Malawi inclusive the levels of investment cannot be financed by the public purse alone. To meet the needs, encouraging private investment in infrastructure is an option that governments cannot afford to ignore. Moreover, private sector participation can bring other benefits than additional capital. The examples include the end-user benefits of a more competitive environment, as well as the mobilisation of the private sector's technological expertise and managerial competences in the public interest.

In other countries private participation in infrastructure has in recent decades helped boost both the coverage and efficiency of infrastructure services. Yet at the same time a number of failed public-private partnerships in the infrastructure sectors attests to the difficult challenges facing policy makers. Infrastructure investment involves contracts which are more complex and of longer duration than in most other parts of the economy, operated under the double imperative of ensuring financial sustainability and meeting user needs and social objectives.

International infrastructure operators are especially sensitive to commercial risks involved in working in unfamiliar local environments and they are also very exposed to public opinion and political scrutiny. The objective of the Principles for Private Sector Participation in Infrastructure is to assist governments that seek private sector involvement in infrastructure development, in attracting investment and mobilising private sector resources for the benefit of society and achieving sustainable development. The Principles are intended as guidance to public authorities contemplating the involvement of private enterprises as one, among several, options to improve the provision of infrastructure services. They shall not be construed as advocating the privatisation or private management of publicly owned infrastructure.

The choice between public and private provision of infrastructure services should be guided by an objective assessment of what best serves the public interest – that is, supports the common well-being. Factors to be taken into account include the current levels of service delivery and the condition of assets, affordability to households and companies, coverage of networks, operational efficiency, long-term maintenance of assets as well as social and environmental sustainability. The decision also needs to be guided by the timeframe in which improvements are required and the sources of finance that are available. The Principles are intended to serve as a first step in the authorities' consideration of private sector participation, offering a coherent catalogue of policy directions to be assessed as part of their development strategies in light of their own national circumstances and needs. The Principles do not aim at detailed prescription or technical advice on implementation of specific aspects of infrastructure investment, contract formulation or regulation.

The Principles can also be used by governments as a template for country self-assessment at national and local government levels, an aid for progress reporting by public authorities, guidance for private enterprises, a tool for structuring regional and other inter-governmental co-operation and public-private dialogues. The Principles cover five important sets of challenges for national authorities. First, the decision to involve the private sector has to be guided by an assessment of the relative long-term costs and benefits and availability of finance, taking into account the pricing of risks transferred to the private operators and prudent fiscal treatment of risks remaining in the public principles for private sector participation in infrastructure. Second, authorities need to ensure an enabling policy framework for investment. Third, the success of private involvement in infrastructure depends on public acceptance and on the capacities at all levels of government to implement agreed projects. A fourth challenge for public authorities and the private sector is to establish a working relationship toward the joint fulfilment of the general public's infrastructure needs. Fifth, as indicated by the last section of the Principles, insofar as they are not rooted in formal legal requirements, governments' expectations regarding responsible business conduct need to be clearly communicated by governments to their private partners. The Principles cannot be seen in isolation. They are intended to be used in conjunction with other OECD policy guidance and tools. The *Policy Framework for Investment* provides a non-prescriptive checklist of issues for consideration by governments engaged in creating an environment that is attractive to domestic and foreign investors and that enhances the benefits of investment to society. O*n Corporate Governance of State-Owned Enterprises* provide recommendations to the state on how to exercise its ownership function *vis-à-vis* state-owned enterprises. Where incumbent utilities providers persist alongside with private participants this is of particular importance. The *Guidelines for Multinational Enterprises* offer recommendations to multinational enterprises operating in or from adhering countries. They provide voluntary principles and standards for responsible business conduct in a variety of areas, most of which are directly relevant to international investors in the infrastructure sector. No exhaustive definition of private sector "participation in infrastructure" is attempted. The Principles are relevant to a range of models of private participation, ranging from relatively limited service and management contracts, to public-private partnerships (PPP), to full or partial public divestiture.

CHAPTER 15

Structure of the Private Sector

THE PRIVATE SECTOR is the part of the economy, sometimes referred to as the citizen sector, which is run by private individuals or groups, usually as a means of enterprise for profit, and is not controlled by the State (areas of the economy controlled by the state being referred to as the he part of the economy that is not state controlled, and is run by individuals and companies for profit. The private sector encompasses all for-profit businesses.

Employment

The private sector employs most of the workforce in some countries. In private sector activities are guided by the motive to earn money.

Regulation

The private sector is legally regulated by the state. Businesses within one country are required to comply with the laws in that country. In some cases, usually involving multinational businesses that can pick and choose their suppliers and locations based on their perception of the regulatory environment, these regulations have resulted in uneven practices within one company. For example, workers in one country may benefit from strong labour unions, while workers in another country have very weak laws supporting labour unions, even though they work for the same employer. In some cases, industries and individual businesses have chosen to self-regulate by applying higher standards for dealing with their workers, customers, or the environment than the minimum that is legally required of them.

Corporate law

Corporate law (also "company" or "corporations" law) is the study of how shareholders, directors, employees, creditors, and other stakeholders such as consumers, the community and the environment interact with one another. Corporate law is a part of a broader companies law (or law of business associations). Other types of business associations can include partnerships or companies limited by guarantee (like some community organizations or charities).

Under corporate law, corporations of all sizes have separate legal personality, with limited or unlimited liability for its shareholders. Shareholders control the company through a board of directors which, in turn, typically delegates control of the corporation's day-to-day operations to a full-time executive. Corporate law deals with firms that are incorporated or registered under the corporate or company law of a sovereign state or their subnational states. The four defining characteristics of the modern corporation are:

- Separate legal personality of the corporation (access to tort and contract law in a manner similar to a person)
- Limited liability of the shareholders (a shareholder's personal liability is limited to the value of their shares in the corporation)
- Shares (if the corporation is a public company, the shares are traded on a stock exchange)
- Delegated management; the board of directors delegates day-to-day management of the company to executives

In many developed countries outside of the English speaking world, company boards are appointed as representatives of both shareholders and employees to "codetermine" company strategy.[2] Corporate law is often divided into corporate governance (which concerns the various power relations within a corporation) and corporate finance (which concerns the rules on how capital is used

Free Enterprise

Capitalism is an economic system based on private ownership of the means of production and their operation for profit Characteristics central to capitalism include private property, capital accumulation, wage labor, voluntary exchange, a price system, and competitive markets.[4][5] In a capitalist market economy, decision-making and investment is determined by the owners of the factors of production in financial and capital markets, and prices and the distribution of goods are mainly determined by competition in the market.

Economists, political economists, and historians have adopted different perspectives in their analyses of capitalism and have recognized various forms of it in practice. These include *laissez-faire* or free market capitalism, welfare capitalism, and state capitalism.

Different forms of capitalism feature varying degrees of free markets, public ownership,[8] obstacles to free competition, and state-sanctioned social policies. The degree of competition in markets, the role of intervention and regulation, and the scope of state ownership vary across different models of capitalism; the extent to which different markets are free, as well as the rules defining private property, are matters of politics and of policy. Most existing capitalist economies are mixed economies, which combine elements of free markets with state intervention, and in some cases, with economic planning. Capitalism has existed under many forms of government, in many different times, places, and cultures. Following the decline of mercantilism, mixed capitalist systems became dominant in the Western world and continue to spread.

Private Enterprise

A privately held company or close corporation is a business company owned either by non-governmental organizations or by a relatively small number of shareholders or company members which does not offer or trade its company stock (shares) to the general public on the stock market exchanges, but rather the company's stock is offered, owned and traded or exchanged privately. More ambiguous terms for a privately held company are unquoted company and unlisted company.

Microeconomics

This aspect of economics deals with the principles of economics that apply to the analysis of the behavior of individual consumers and businesses in the economy. Microeconomics is the branch of economics that analyzes the market behavior of individual consumers and firms in an attempt to understand the decision-making process of firms and households. This means that individuals and firms in an economy form microeconomics since that state forms macroeconomics.

CHAPTER 16

Creating Vibrant Private Sector Reforms

PRIVATE SECTOR REFORMS HAVE TO BE THOUGHT PROPERLY at both central and local government. There are two basic ideas on which most reforms have been based in Malawi. First, is that public spending should be reduced, either absolutely or as a proportion of national product. Second, markets are good and if a market style of relationship is possible then it should be introduced. As earlier indicated values required to run public services are often different from those required to run a successful business. Values of equity and justice play a part in the public sector. The task is rarely based on the need to attract customers. Prices are rarely set to maximize profits or market share. Investments are rarely based on prospective profits. According to Morgan {2009} PSM interventions tend to be conscious of process, preferring methods that encourage beneficiaries to be initiators of development, participants in the process of development are transmitters of skills and knowledge, rather than passive recipients. The influence of market-based paradigm is most evident in civil service reform discussions and accountability, where market principles are employed in the interests of performance and less attention is given to human considerations {Sorokou 2005}.

Additionally how it (the public sector) has evolved from being a centralized instrument of the state to decentralization and the many reform challenges that are encountered in this evolution. It endeavors to discuss the structures, processes and politics of the public sector and how various actors therein influence change and reform that affect the welfare of people and society in Africa in general and in Malawi in particular. This would require an understanding of intellectual roots, structures, principles, processes and functions of a vibrant economic system that would bring wealth to our nation.

This knowledge and understanding will enable all the three players in economy to skillfully operate and execute their duties within the board policy framework of modern government structures and organizations and to be able to follow the complex processes and politics that form the gamut of such institutions in society.

Shim {2009} says series of practical and proven methods that work for wealth creation through a vibrant economic system at these three levels have been presented. Many countries all over the world now begin to understand the unique role a vibrant economic system plays in an economy that can contribute to a wealth creation.

The Private Sector Development Reform Programme (PSDRP)

Private Sector Development (PSD) is a term in the international development industry to refer to a range of strategies for promoting economic growth and reducing poverty in developing countries by building private enterprises. This could be through working with firms directly, with membership organisations to represent them, or through a range of areas of policy and regulation to promote functioning, competitive markets. This could be the framework of the Government of the Republic of Malawi which would aim at reducing the cost of doing business in the country by encouraging competitiveness in the private sector. PSDRP would aim at fast tracking and accelerate private sector reforms in a number of key sectors which are expected to lead to an improved competitive business environment. with the purpose of promoting investment in the private business sector. The cost of doing business in Malawi is too high, effecting foreign and domestic investment.

The PSD would be a collaboration between the Malawian government and the private sector, promoting quality of service and private investment by addressing numerous issues involving finances, infrastructure, and bureaucracy. Some of the PSD initiatives recent successes include reducing the amount of time it takes to register a company, speeding up the border clearance time, and a large reduction in the number of licenses required to start and operate a business in Malawi. These are just the beginning of the PSD initiative's projects to bolster the private business sector in Malawi, transforming this country's promising resources into a worldwide market for quality goods and services.

Policy Actions and Priority Areas

While fundamental reforms have modernized the environment for doing business in Malawi, more is to be done to improve the quality of the country's investment climate. A business environment that supports private sector-led growth is the key to long-term sustainable poverty reduction. This is a call to implement fundamental reforms that would modernize the environment for doing business in the country with some far-reaching reforms. This private sector assessment (PSA) analyzes the reforms to date and suggests further policy actions and priorities in the areas of:

- Business law reform,
- Promoting economic opportunities for both men and women,
- Infrastructure,
- State-owned enterprises,
- The tax system, and
- The financial system.

The policy recommendations in the PSA provide the basis for discussions between the Government of the private sector. This would ensure that the private sector, and other stakeholders regarding future reform priorities that will contribute to the country's resources should be used most productively.

Liberalization, Civil Society and the Media

Neo-liberalism demands that not only the public sector should play a key role in public governance and development processes. The liberalization of economic and political space has therefore given rise to the role of non-governmental organizations (NGOs), civil society, the media and other non-state actors in public governance and development processed. There is no single definition of the civil society, however, that is acceptable to everybody. In fact, there are as many definitions of civil society as there are people.

What is generally agreeable, however, is that civil society is that space, institution, social process and interaction above the individual and yet below the state. Wiseman Chirwa (2002) offers two approaches used when looking at the civil society as an institution and civil society as a process of human interactions. As an institution, civil society is defined as an informal or formal institution whose members are engaged primarily in a complex of activities outside the state structures.

These activities may include economic, social and cultural production, voluntary association and household life, which either preserve or transform the institution's identity and exert pressure or controls on the state structures. Such activities allow the people outside government or state structures to interact with each other and with those in government and state echelons. It is because of this role that the media is perceived as part of civil society, which connects people with government.

The media exposes to the people what government is doing with the mandate the people gave it and takes information about people feelings, views and attitudes regarding their government to the government. As a process of human interactions, civil society is defined as an organized social life standing between the individual and state. It is the process that connects the individual with the state. A political side of society where entertainment, conflicts and conflict resolutions and negotiations take place; information is passed and values are learnt.

Civil society, in this sense, is more than mere physical place as it encompasses a process of human interactions. Civil society organizations can also be developmental, issue-centered, interest-based and/or just spiritual or religious in nature. Because of this diversity, civil society is seen as providing good ground for the consolidation of a culture of pluralism in many democratic and developmental aspects. The opening up of a civil space implies that the public sector now faces competition from other actors and stakeholders involved in public affairs. It is argued that competition, checks and balances posed by plurality of actors is an incentive for the public sector to move towards tenets of good governance; accountability, efficiency and effectiveness in its activities.

Part VI
STAKEHOLDER MANAGEMENT

CHAPTER 17

The Nature of Stakeholder Management

What Stakeholder Management is all about?

THE STAKEHOLDER MANAGEMENT focuses on the recognition of the contribution that individual stakeholders make towards the value creation activities of an organization. According to Khomba {2016:14} each stakeholder will have an interest or stake in the running of an organization and actively contribute towards its financial and corporate sustainability. Stakeholder management is the process by which an organisation involves people who may be affected by the decisions it makes or can influence the implementation of its decisions. For example shareholders provide equity capital, customers offer money in exchange for goods or services, employees provide labour, government provides business infrastructure, business financing and legislation, competitions provide data information for bench marking and product continuous improvement, the local community provides labour and final consumers, and the natural environment and suppliers provide raw materials and inputs for production.

From the above discussion it shows that stakeholder management is a critical component to the successful delivery of any project, programme or activity. A stakeholder in this case is any individual, group or organization that can affect, be affected by, or perceive itself to be affected by a programme. Effective Stakeholder Management creates positive relationships with stakeholders through the appropriate management of their expectations and agreed objectives. Stakeholder management is a process and control that must be planned and guided by underlying principles. Stakeholder management within businesses, organizations, or projects prepares a strategy utilizing information (or intelligence) gathered during the following common processes.

According to Stovall {2004} it is also based on the stakeholder perspective that it is equitable that corporate wealth should flow to those who create it based upon all forms of contributions and not just the initial input of financial capital provided. According to Khomba {2011} established that 74.4% of organizations recognize the interdependence of efforts and rewards among their stakeholders and that 69.7% of respondents ensure that all stakeholders receive sufficient benefits to ensure their collaboration with their organizations. This means that the stakeholder perspective is consistent with the team solidarity and sharing phenomena.

In what follows are the perspectives presented in Figure 2 below.

Figure 16:1 Stakeholder Management Model

Source: Ngwira {2014

Understanding Key Stakeholders

There is now need to know more about your key stakeholders. You need to know how they are likely to feel about and react to your project. You also need to know how best to engage them in your project and how best to communicate with them. Key questions that can help you understand your stakeholders are:

- What financial or emotional interest do they have in the outcome of your work? Is it positive or negative?
- What motivates them most of all?
- What information do they want from you?
- How do they want to receive information from you? What is the best way of communicating your message to them?
- What is their current opinion of your work? Is it based on good information?
- Who influences their opinions generally, and who influences their opinion of you? Do some of these influencers therefore become important stakeholders in their own right?
- If they are not likely to be positive, what will win them around to support your project?[9]
- If you don't think you will be able to win them around, how will you manage their opposition?
- Who else might be influenced by their opinions? Do these people become stakeholders in their own right?

State of the Nation Assignments

- Communicate: To ensure intended message is understood and the desired response achieved.
- Consult, early and often: To get the useful information and ideas, ask questions.
- Remember, they are human: Operate with an awareness of human feelings.
- Plan it: Time investment and careful planning against it, has a significant payoff.
- Relationship: Try to engender trust with the stakeholders.
- Simple but not easy: Show your care. Be empathetic. Listen to the stakeholders.
- Managing risk: Stakeholders can be treated as risk and opportunities that have probabilities and impact.

- Compromise: Compromise across a set of stakeholders' diverging priorities.
- Understand what is success: Explore the value of the project to the stakeholder.
- Take responsibility: Project governance is the key of project success

Strengthening Sound Financial Reporting Systems for Stakeholders

Khomba {2016:27} points out that as experienced from the failures of the Government IFMIS, the Public Finance Management Systems and the financial management systems in the private sector, it becomes necessary and prudent that robust and water – tight financial reporting systems are developed and implemented to detect, prevent and monitor fraud at all levels. The thinking is that this would help serve different stakeholders efficiently and effectively. As the resources are preserved, they can be channeled towards strategic and well meaning intervention that will ultimately help improve the welfare of ordinary citizens {Khomba 2016:27}.

CHAPTER 18

Stakeholder Analysis

IT IS WELL ACKNOWLEDGED that any given organization will have multiple stakeholders including, but not limited to, customers, shareholders, employees, management of institutions, suppliers, community at large and so forth. Within the field of marketing, it is believed that customers are one of the most important stakeholders for managing its long-term value, with a firm's major objective being the management of customer satisfaction. This means that the public sector should operate as if it is in the private sector.

Strategic Moves for Stakeholders

he first step in the strategic move for stakeholders is to brainstorm who your stakeholders are. As part of this, think of all the people who are affected by your work, who have influence or power over it, or have an interest in its successful or unsuccessful conclusion. Remember that although stakeholders may be both organizations and people, ultimately you must communicate with people. Make sure that you identify the correct individual stakeholders within a stakeholder organization. So in a nutshell, the stakeholder management comprises four steps, which are below:

- Identify, recognize and acknowledge stakeholder;
- Determine their influence and interest;
- Establish communication management plan
- Influencing and engaging stakeholder

Prioritize Your Stakeholders

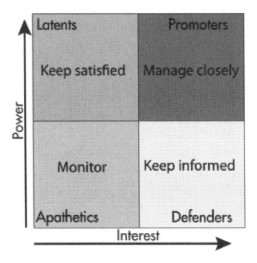

Figure 17:1: A stakeholders matrix showing which strategic moves to use.

Source: Clarke, et al {2007}

You may now have a long list of people and organizations that are affected by your work. Some of these may have the power either to block or advance. Some may be interested in what you are doing, others may not care. Map out your stakeholders on a Power/Interest Grid as shown by the image, and classify them by their power over your work and by their interest in your work. There are other tools available to map out your stakeholders and how best to influence then.

For example, your boss is likely to have high power and influence over your projects and high interest. Your family may have high interest, but are unlikely to have power over it. Someone's position on the grid shows you the actions you have to take with them:

- **High power, interested people:** these are the people you must fully engage and make the greatest efforts to satisfy.
- **High power, less interested people:** put enough work in with these people to keep them satisfied, but not so much that they become bored with your message.

- **Low power, interested people:** keep these people adequately informed, and talk to them to ensure that no major issues are arising. These people can often be very helpful with the detail of your project.
- **Low power, less interested people:** again, monitor these people, but do not bore them with excessive communication.

Engaging and Communicating with Stakeholders

With a clear understanding of Stakeholders, engaging and communicating can be achieved through a variety of channels based upon who the stakeholder is.

- **High power, interested people:** Manage closely. Best channels: Issue, Change Logs, Status Meetings
- **High power, less interested people:** Keep satisfied. Best channels: Steering Committee, Board **Low power, interested people:** Keep informed. Best channels: In-Person, Video, Email Updates
- **Low power, less interested people:** Monitor. Best channels: Send Email, Status Reports

Stakeholder Analysis: Mind mapping tool

Stakeholder Analysis template created using a mindmapping tool. The first four branches organise stakeholders into the impact and influence groupings, and stakeholders are then mapped by adding branches to each group. Using a mindmap is a great way of analysing stakeholders and many mindmapping tools have collaboration options which allow multiple people to work on an analysis. Figure 17.2 below illustrates the mind map.

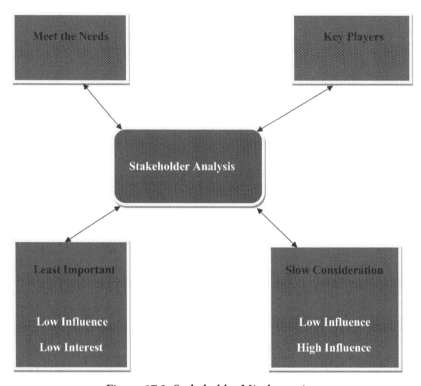

Figure 17.2: Stakeholder Mindmapping

Source: Mindmeister.com.

Once you have mapped your stakeholders you can focus your efforts on the high priority groups while providing sufficient information to keep the less powerful groups happy.

CHAPTER 19

Strategic Management for the Private and Public Sector

What Strategic Management is all about?

Strategic Management is a stream of decisions and actions that leads to the development of an effective strategy or strategies to help achieve corporate objectives. Strategic Management is the way in which successful executives formulate and implement strategies to achieve goals and other objectives of their organizations. Strategic Management is concerned with deciding on a strategy and planning how that strategy is to be put into effect. Peter Drucker states that the task of thinking through the mission of the business that is asking the question, what is our business and what should it be? is critical to managing organizations.

This leads to the setting of objectives, the development of strategies and plans, making the decisions for tomorrow's results in a changing environment. The business environment is constantly changing and executive managers are increasingly exposed to new challenges in the operations of organizations. The operating environment has become ever more volatile as modern economies have emerged {David, 2011}.

Khomba {2016} modern industries cannot afford to be static and mechanistic as there are constant rapid technology changes, there has been a shift to more knowledge-work based management systems; there is currently an increased emphasis on corporate citizenship in respect of social responsibility and corporate conscience issues and more importantly, industries have to address the problems of environmental degradation and global warming challenges.

Strategic Management is a continuous process of making entrepreneurial decisions systematically and with the best possible knowledge of (a) futurity (b) organizing systematically the effort needed to carry out decisions and (c) measuring the results against expectations through organized systematic feedback. At the heart of Strategic Management is the formulation of strategy and strategic decisions which aim at achieving some advantage for the organization over competition. Strategy can be seen as a search for strategic fit with the business environment. This could mean major resource shifts or changes in an organization for example decision to reposition one in the market. Strategy also creates opportunities by building on an organization's resources and competences. This is called the resource based view of strategy.

Strategy and Strategic Decisions

Strategy is the direction and scope of an organization over the long term which achieves advantage in a changing environment through its configuration of resources and competences with the objective of fulfilling stakeholder expectations. Strategic decisions are about the long term direction of an organization. Thus they are likely to be complex in nature since they are made under conditions of uncertainty.

Strategic Position

Understanding the strategic position is concerned with identifying the impact on strategy of the external environment an organization's strategic capability resources and competencies) and the expectations and influence of stakeholders. Environment: The organization exists in the context of a complex political social technological environment. Thos environment is dynamic and more complex in other organizations than others. These challenges lead to opportunities and threats on an organization

Influences of expectations on an organization's purposes are and corporate governance are crucial in strategic positioning important. For instance who should the organization serve/ how should managers be held responsible. Note that the expectations of various stakeholders also affect purposes. Who prevails depends on who has the greatest power. Cultural influences from within the organization and around the world also influence the strategy and organization follows.

Strategic Capability

This is made up of resources and competencies. Can think about this by considering strengths and weaknesses (whether its is a competitive advantage /disadvantage). The aim is to form a view of the internal influences and constraints on strategic choices for the future. It is usually what we call core competencies, a combination of resources and high levels of competence that provide advantages which competitors find difficult to imitate.

Strategic Choice

Involves understanding the underlying bases for future strategy at both the business and corporate levels and the options for developing strategy in both the directions in which strategy might move and methods of development. There are strategic choices in terms of how the organization seeks to compete at business level. This involves the identification of a basis for competitive advantage. This arises from an understanding of the markets, customers and strategic capability of the organization. At the highest level there are issues of corporate level strategy. These are concerned with the scope of an organization's strategies. It includes decisions about portfolio of products and or business and spread of markets. For most organizations international strategy are a key a part of corporate level strategy. Parenting is part of this strategy. It involves the relationship between separate parts of the business and how the corporate parent adds value to these parts e.g. exploring synergies within an organization that can add value.

Strategy Implementation

Translating strategy into action is concerned with ensuring that strategies are working in practice. This means that the execution of strategic process involves the translation of plans into action. Organizations get inputs from their environment in the form of financial capital from shareholders, debt capital from financiers, labour capital from the local community and labour markets, and natural resource capital from the natural environment {Khomba 2016}.

Structuring an organization to support performance includes organizational structure, processes and relationships. Enabling success through the way in which separate resources of an organization support strategies. Through their internal business processes, organization process transform these inputs into finished or semi-finished goods or services. During the implementation process, organizations are supposed to use their resources in the most economic, efficient and effective manner.

Managing strategy involves change most often. Many business managers say that modern business practices also dictate that firms have to be ethical in their undertakings. For example industrial enterprises have an ethical duty to protect the environment against degradation and pollution. Additionally once the goods and services are produced they are given back to the environment through customers and consumers for final consumption, there by completing the ecosystem.

Evaluation and Control

This involves checking results whether the objectives are met. Corrective actions are made based on variances or standard deviations. Many business commentators say that corporate performance is the managers' ability to compare actual results to the plans that were drawn to originally address the strategic vision, mission and value statements of an organization. After developing plans in the course of the budgeting process, managers can compare actual results against the set targets to measure performance with regard to various activities and the overall organization. Khmba {2016} points out that Malawi and indeed the entire African continent have unique problems that need unique solutions. There is need to understand the business dynamics, relevance and applicability of the business models being in place within the sectors.

Conclusion

This book in summary points out that Malawi needs a vibrant economic system that would create its own wealth. As stated earlier it is envisaged that if the principles and concepts presented based on the findings of my research the economy of our nation will enjoy wealth and will become wealthy. This means that our Gross Domestic Product {GDP} will start to promise and this will see all the players in an economy which are the individuals [Households], firms and the state start experiencing the economic growth.

Over the past few years, Malawi has been witnessing slow down of business transactions and massive closures of some of its very important companies, especially in the manufacturing sector. Regrettably, the economy has been witnessing a great deal of so many ills and evils that include layoffs of the working class people, low purchasing power amongst consumers due to the continued depression of the Kwacha, high interest and inflation rates, high rates of insecurity, low tax collections and huge government borrowings and more companies, especially the SMEs even closing {Khomba 2016:46}. To sum up it all the following four policy challenges: the exchange rate, natural resource management, structural transformation and employment are strangulating and dogging Malawi.

The strategic approaches such as implementation of the wealth creation model, move from free market to mixed economy, move from public administration to new public management, enhancing the private sector through government support, financing the public sector through equity finance and move towards abandoning donor dependency in a long term, creating vibrant private sector reforms as well as stakeholder management and the turnaround strategies presented in this book could serve as solution to these challenges.

References

Burgess S.M., (2005) The importance and motivational content of money attitudes. South Africa with Living standards similar to those in industrialized. *South Africa Journal of Psychology*

Carsky, M.L., & McLaughlin, G.W.,(1984) Change in consumer competency and attitude Dostudent characteristics make different? *Proceedings of the American Councilon Consumer Inter ests, USA,30,166-173.*

Chenhall, R.H., (2005) integrative strategic performance measurement systems strategic alignment of manufacturing. Leaning and strategic outcomes: an exploratory study, accounting, organizational and society, vol.30,pp.395-422.

Clarke, M.D, Heaton M.B., Isaraelsen C.L &Eggett D.L (2005) Theacquisition of family financial rolesand responsibilities. *Family and consumer sciences Research Journal,33,321*-340.http//doi.org/10.1177/107 7727x0424117

Dennis, H. Migliaccio, J (1997) Redefiningrement: The baby boomer challenge. *Generations Summer,45-50*

David, F., (2011) Strategic Management: concepts & case studies. Upper saddle rivenj: prentice hall.

Debuskg, K., and Crabtree, A.D., (2006) Does the balanced scoredcard improve performance?' management "library management, vol.3l3,pp 162-168.

Edwards, R. and Allen M. & Hayhoe, C., (2007) Financial attitudes and family communication about students finances: Theroleofsex differences. *Communication Report*

Glass, J.C., & Kilpatrick, B., (1998) Gender comparisons of baby boomer sand final preparation for retirement. Educational Gerontology

Gregoire., T. K., Kily K., & Richardson, V., (2002). Gender and racialine qualities in retire mentre sources Journal of Women and Aging

Hanafizadeh, P., and Sorousha, M., (2008) "A methodology to define strategic processes organization: an exploration study in managerial holding companies" business process management journal.Vol.14 no2,pp.219-227.

Kayuni, K.M, and Tambulasi, R.I.C., (2012) Ubuntu and corporate social responsibility: the case of selected Malawian organizations"; Africa journal of economic and management studies, vol.3 no.1,pp.64-76

Kemp, C.L., & Denton, M (2003). The allocation of responsibility for later life: Canadian reflection sontheroleso find individuals, government, employer sand families. Ageing and Society,23(6),737-760.http.\\dx.doi.org/10.1017/So144686X03001363

Khomba. J., kangaude - ulayaec 7 hanifrc 92012) crafting a sustainable corporate performance: the value of corporate stakeholders" Australian journal of business and management research,6(12):20-27

Khomba, J.K, Sankhulani E.J., Kangaude – Ulaya, E.C., & Hanifrc 92013)" crafting business ethic and corporate governance in Malawi: the value of an Africa ubuthu philosophy" Australian journal of business and management research,2(12)

Khomba J.K., (2015a)" Conceptualization of the balance scorecard (bsc) model: a critical review on its validity in Africa"; international journal of commerce and management, 25(4):424-441.

Khomba, J.K., (2015b) "Use of traditional financial measurement systems: a critical assessment on their application validity" journal of financial of reporting and accounting

Khombajk, Vermaak FNS &gouws dg (2015)" relevance of the balanced scorecard model: value – driven?" European journal of business and social science, 4(2): 74-97

Khombajk, vermaakjfns&hanif (2012) "relevance of the balanced scorecard model in Africa shareholder –centered of stakeholder –centered/' Africa journal of business management, (6917): 5773-5785.

Koster, J.D., (1996), managing the transformation: in citizen participation in local government, bekker(ed), j.l van schaik, Pretoria (pp99-188).

Laudon, K.C., and Laudon (2012) essential of management information systems: managing a digit firm.prentice hall, new jersey USA.M & T

Lee Ronald, Andwer, M.,& Timothy M.(2003) Life Cycle Saving and the Demographic Transition: The Case of Taiwan.Inc. Chu & R. Lee (Eds),

Lyons, A.C, Schrempf E.& Roberts, H. (2006).FinancialEducation and Communication between parents and children. *Journal of Consumer Education*,23,64-76

Martin A. & Oliva, J.C (2001). Teaching children about money. Application of social learning and cog native learning developmental theories.*Journal of family& Consumer Science*,93(2)26-29

Mc Donald, D.(2002) T.S., *Creaders shine on financial literacy quiz*. Retried from http: www.thestreet.com / funds/ deardagen/9203371.html

Moeller, k (2009) intangible and financial performance: causes and effects: Journal of intellectual capital, vol.10,no 2pp.224-245.

Moloketi, G.R., (2009) towards a common understanding of corruption in Africa: public policy and administration, vol.24no,3pp331-338.

Morgan, G. K., and Mirvis P.(2009) Leading corporate citizen: governance, structure systems" corporate governance, vol9,no.1,pp39-49

Neely A., Gregory., M., and K., (1995) performance measurement system design: a literature review and research agenda "international journal of operations and production management, vol.15,no 4,pp 80-166.

Newberts. L., (2003) Realizing the sprit and impact of adm smith's capitalism through entrepreneurship 'journal of business ethics, vol.46, no.3,pp.25

Niven, P.R. (2008), Balance scorecard step by step for government and nonprofit agencies(2)edition), john Wiley and sons, new york

Norvilitis, J.M., Merwin, M.M, Osberg, T.M.,Roehling, P.V.,Young, P.,& Kamas, M.M(2006).Personality factors, money attitudes, financial knowledge, and credit card debt in college students. Journal of applied social Psychology, 36(6),1395http:\\dx.doi.org/10.11 1\ jon.0021-9029.2006.00065.x

Ngwira, K.P, (2012) Conceptual frame work of Wealth of Nations, Author House, Bloomington

Ngwira, K.P.,(2012) Circular Flow of Gross Domestic Product (GDP) Author House, Bloomington

Ngwira K.P, (2012) Wealth Creation Model, Author House, Bloomington

Ngwira, K.P.,(2014) Stakeholder Management Model, Author House, Blooming

Ngwira, K.P.,(2012) Conceptual Frame Work of Wealth of Nations, Author House, Bloomington

Ngwira, K.P.,(2016) Journal Article of the Role of Public Procurement in Malawi, Author House, Bloomington

Ngwira, K.P.,(2016) Journal Article of Quality Assurance for Higher Education Institutions in Malawi, Author House, Bloomington

Ngwira, K.P.,(2016) Journal Article:Learn the skills you will need to start and grow a successful business, Author House, Bloomington

Ngwira, K.P.,(2016) Journal Article: The Role of Anti-Corruption Bureu in Malawi, Author House, Bloomington

Ngwira, K.P.,(2016) Journal Article: Employment Practices in Malawi, Author House, Bloomington

Ngwira, K.P.,(2016)*Journal Article: The Role of Taxation in Malawi*, Author House, Bloomington

Ngwira, K.P., (2016) *Journal Article: Evaluation of Bids for public procurement Entities in Malawi*, Author House, Bloomington

Ngwira, K.P., (2016) *Journal Article: The Role of Anti-Corruption Bureau in Malawi* 'Author House Bloomington

Ngwira, K.P., (2016) *Journal Article: Employment practices in in Malawi*, Author House Bloomington

Ngwira, K.P., (2016) *Journal Article: Preparation of Bidding Documents for Goods, and Routine* Service for Public Entities in Malawi, Author House Bloomington

Rasche, A., and Esserd. E. (2006) From stakeholder management to stakeholder accountability: applying habermasiam discourse ethic to accountability research" journal of business ethis, vol.65.pp.251-267.

Rossouw, D.J., (2009) the ethics of corporate governance global convergence or divergence?' international journal of law and management, vol.51,nol, pp.43-51

Saunders, M., Lewis, P. and Thorn hill, A. (2003), research methods for business students, prentice hall Edinburgh, England

Rettig, K.D.(1985) Consumer socialization in the family. *Journal of consumer Education*, 3,1-7

Roberts, J.A. & Jones, E. (2001) Money attitudes, credit carduse, and compulsive buying among America *college student. The journal of Consumer Affairs.*

Schellenberg, G. (1994).The Road to Retirement. Ottawa. Centre for International Statistics, Canadian Councilon Social Development

Shim, S. Xio, J.J., Barber, B.L., & Lyons, A.C., (2009) Path way life success: A conceptual model of financial well-being for young adults. *Journal of Applied Development Psychology,*30(6), 708htt:dx.doi.org/10.1016/j. appdev.2009.02.003

Sorokou, C.F., & Weissbrod, C.S. (2005) Men and women's attachment and contact patterns with parents during the first year of college. *Journal of Youth and Adolescence,*34(3)221-228.www.ccsenet.org/ibr International Business Research Vol.7,No.6:2014

Szwajkowaki, E., (2000) 'Simplifying the principles of stakeholder management: the three most important principles", business and society, vol39 no4,pp.379-396

About The Author

Dr. Kingstone P. Ngwira, an author of international bestselling books: Doing Business God's Way; Quality Insurance for Higher Education Institutions in Malawi and the Road to Entrepreneurship is an Apostle by calling is an insightful teacher, motivational speaker, the President and Senior Pastor of Pentecostal Life Church International (PLCI) with a network of churches in Malawi and other parts of Africa.

He has a God given mandate, "To raise a generation that will serve God with excellence and empower them to do exploits to their world". As an educationist, his mission currently pioneers the establishment of educational institutions of higher learning such as Exploits University (EU) and Pentecostal Life University (PLU) in Malawi where he serves as the Chancellor.

Additionally, Dr. Kingstone P. Ngwira is founder/Chairman for Pentecostal Live Radio and TV Stations where he hosts programs, "Radio and TV Pulpit"," Business Coach" and "Christian Talk Point." He is blessed with two children: Pastor Prince and Gift and married to Late Pastor Martha who was Chief Executive Officer of Dominion Foundation Limited.

Printed in the United States
By Bookmasters